PERRY POWER

Breaking The Silence

Stories From Survivors Of Sexual Abuse

Second edition

This book was professionally typeset on Reedsy.
Find out more at reedsy.com

Contents

Introduction

I want to start by saying that the journey of overcoming abuse is different for everyone. What might work for someone may not work for you. However, the focus of me putting this together is not necessarily about how to deal with, or how to overcome your abuse for the long term, but more so taking ownership of your story and breaking your silence. I truly believe that the power of breaking your silence is truly transformational for everyone who does it.

You'll find that this book is more of a guide. There are questions and exercises for you to complete along the way, so feel free to follow along. As well as a guide, it serves as a platform for both victims and survivors of sexual abuse. There are stories of 14 survivors in this book. Some of them are breaking their silence for the first time, whilst for some, they have already shared it before. The whole notion behind these stories is to simply give you permission to share yours. It's to show you that you aren't alone. It's to show you that there are many people out there just like you who lived in silence, and hopefully, with you seeing their brave souls breaking their silence, you can do the same.

It's to turn you from a victim to a survivor.

Thank You

For every brave soul who broke their silence and shared their story inside this book, thank you. If it weren't for you and your bravery, this book would not be in the hands of those who need to hear it most.

And to those of you that become the 15th survivor inside this book, this couldn't be done without you either.

Keep soldiering on.

Prologue

It's the 16th of February, 3 days before the release of this book, and I was frustrated. In fact, I was more than frustrated. I was furious. I had just moved to Guildford and I still had no idea what I was going to do. I had left my old business behind because I felt like I was operating out of alignment, and I committed myself fully to making my vision happen. Yet, I didn't know what the next step was. And it was annoying because it's in my nature to control things. But I was forcing myself to let go of the need to control and just allow the universe to align itself accordingly. I'm lying in bed thinking about what I could do next to get my message of #breakthesilence out there, and it dawned on me that I had already written a book which is just sitting on my Google Drive. So I had a conversation with the voice inside my head (which we all have) and asked it a few questions...

Perry: "Why haven't we done anything with the book yet?"

Voice: "Because we need to hire a book coach to get it done. We also need an editor, a designer, and then we need to pitch it to publishers. And we don't have the $5k - $10k to do this."

Perry: "Why do we need to do all of this?"

Voice: "Don't you want it to be perfect and be sitting in book stores?"

Perry: "Sure, that would be great. But wanting it to be perfect has already delayed this book from getting out there by a year. How many lives could this have impacted already?"

Voice: "Well- "

Perry: "We believe in the universe right? How about this. Let's install Grammarly and spell check the book. Let's then grab a headshot from our latest photoshoot and design the cover in Canva. And then we stick this bad boy on Amazon KDP and self-publish it. If this was meant to be the way all along, then we'll see it take off. If not, we'll see that too. What do we have to lose?"

So I got to work and 3 days later this book was out there. As I write this it's been a little over 3 months since it's been out, and would you like to know the results? I'll assume that's a yes...

- Sold over 700 copies of the book
- #1 on Amazon US (Sexual Abuse category)
- #1 on Amazon UK (Mental Health category)
- TEDx talk titled 'Breaking Your Silence'
- Exclusive article in The Sun (online)
- Featured article in the Bracknell News (online)
- Frontpage of the Bracknell News (paper)
- Featured article in MyLondon (online)
- Featured article in the Surrey Advertiser (online)
- Frontpage of the Surrey Advertiser (paper)
- Two women on Tinder said that they have read my book as

their opening message (I'm dead serious lol)
- A member of staff at the Ministry Of Justice reached out to me and thanked me for putting this book out there

This all happened within the last 3 months. No prior marketing. No build-up. No paid press releases. Crazy right? I'm not saying any of this to impress. Please don't think that I am. I'm just trying to show you what can happen when you just do it. Because I spent a whole year pushing this book back because I believed everything needed to be perfect before putting it out there. Or did I? Well, here's the thing about perfectionism. Perfectionism is just a bunch of insecurities. I was insecure about putting this book out there. One because it's an extension of me. And two, because I didn't want it to be received badly (or not to be received at all). But once I did it, everything clicked into place.

When my book was released and the press started to pick it up, I knew at some stage the family of my step-grandad would see it. We haven't had contact with them for over 15 years (since he passed away), and I just had a feeling that would soon change. But I'll tell you this, I wasn't looking forward to it. Only because I had already pictured in my mind how it would play out. I pictured a member of his family seeing my story online and become furious over what I was saying. Because as far as I was aware, my step-grandad only abused members of my family, not his. Meaning that his family had no idea of the type of man that he was. So I was anticipating a flood of threats from them and a lot of anger. A couple of weeks go by and I see a message in my Facebook Messenger Outbox. Here's the opening of the message (Note: They aren't yet in a place to disclose what relation they have to my step-grandad. So, therefore, I'll just say 'family member'. All you need to know is that they're blood-related and were very close):

"Hello Perry, this is a very hard message for me to write. I came across your page whilst looking for your aunt on Facebook. You won't remember me, but I am (family member)."

I couldn't continue reading this message because my heart sunk. It felt like all the walls were closing in on me. I knew my story would get onto their radar eventually, but I didn't know it would be so soon. But what's done is done. They've already read my story and messaged me. There's nothing I can do about that. So I pick my phone back up and read the rest of the message...

And I couldn't believe it.

This person tells me they are shocked to hear about what happened to me and that I have their full support in what I'm doing. She further goes on to tell me that members of their family were abused by him too...

I was in utter shock. I had no idea he abused members of his own family too. And the fact they have reached out to me to connect was something I could have never imagined. After a bit of back and forth, I suggested they read this book. I pre-warned them it would be hard to read, primarily because my story is about someone close to them. However, as they were victims too, I thought it would be worth it.

A couple of weeks later we suggested it would be good to meet up and clear the air. So my cousin and I met up with the two girls in a park and chatted. We were there for hours. We talked. We hugged. We cried. We vented. And we laughed. I found out more about my step-grandad's school he was raised in and the abuse he endured. I felt the girl's pain and discomfort when they described what he would do to them growing up. And I saw just how powerful breaking the silence can be.

Because here's the thing. If I had never broken my silence, they would have never read my story and we would never have met up. If I had never found forgiveness, I wouldn't have allowed myself to see them either. One of the girls even said to me that they were surprised I had replied to their original message. She thought I might not have wanted to hear from them, which is linked to the shame they still carry (which is common amongst victims of sexual abuse). But we met up and rekindled a loving relationship between two families. Now they are supporting me with everything I'm doing here.

As unexpected as this was, it was one of the most profound experiences ever.

Whilst I will talk a little later about the potential outcomes from breaking your silence, I want to say right now that really, at the end of the day, you never know. I had no idea this was going to happen. And whilst I know I'm very fortunate for this to have been the response I had gotten, I also know there are people out there for which aren't so lucky. But that should never stop you from moving forward, taking action, and breaking your silence.

Because again, it's the land of the unknown. You'll drive

yourself crazy thinking of the million and one possibilities of what may or may not happen. But what you can do is control what happens right now in the present moment.

And that's you breaking your silence. To yourself first and then to others. Because breaking your silence needs to be for you, and you alone.

It's been a wild ride so far since launching BTS, both personally and out there in the world with you guys.
And I'm looking forward to seeing what happens next.

I

PART 1. MY STORY

The Innocent Childhood

I'm a city boy, born and raised in London (although having grown much older, I can confidently say that I'm now a country boy. Give me land, a tractor, and some wood to chop and I'm happy).

My mum walked out and left when I was 4, leaving my dad to raise me on his own. He was an incredible man. He did everything he could to give me a life that he never had growing up. He would spoil me with gifts because he never had any. He would spoil me with holidays because he never went away, and he would make sure that he was always there for me. Which was great, but it also had its drawbacks. My dad was the son of alcoholic parents. Growing up, he would come home from school, clean the house, get the shopping in and prepare dinner for when his mum and stepdad got home from the pub. Completely drunk out of their minds was a regular sight for him. My dad never experienced love growing up. He would often tell me that if he never came home for a couple of days, his parents wouldn't be out looking for him. They'd be too drunk to. The only thing they'd notice was that their dinner wasn't cooked and ready on the table. So because of this, my dad showed his love towards me in a way he never received. He would want the contact details of all my friends, he would want the address of the house I was going to and he would give me a specific time to be home by. He contained me inside a bubble and did not give me much room to venture out. This is why as soon as I could when I was 18/19 years old, I left home. I went to University and then traveled around Australia. I needed to venture out and make my own mistakes without my dad breathing down my neck all the time.

A couple of years after my mum walked out (for anyone who is wondering, we have a great relationship now), my dad met a woman for which they shortly after married. My stepmum is South African, so the wedding happened over in SA and I was the best man. Yep, the best man ladies and gents. I walked down the aisle, handed over the rings, and ran the show like a complete boss. I think I was 7 or 8 years old, maybe 9. I can't exactly remember. What I can remember was the hot sun beaming down, Great British flags waving, the horse and carriage, and the happy faces - it was beautiful. We used to go to South Africa nearly every year to visit my grandparents. Some of my happiest memories are over there. If you are a fan of a good sunset, then you won't see much better than at the Kruger National Park.

Whilst at primary school, my Aunty (dad's sister) would come and collect me after school every day. We had a super close relationship, we still do in fact. She'd bring me back to hers where I would stay and watch TV, or play with my cousin (who is nearly 10 years older than me and is like a sister). My cousin and I used to hang out a lot growing up. Her friends were my friends. I was there for the laughs. I was there for the cries. I was there when she got beat up by two girls (they were bullies) and I stood there terrified. And I was there when she brought a new life into this world, who is the cutest and most adorable boy you'll ever meet. He is very cheeky though, I can't ignore that fact. But nonetheless, I'm super close with them. My cousin and I would often go and visit our nan and grandad, who lived a 15-minute walk away. Our nan used to call me 'Spike' because of my hedgehog-like hair as a kid, and my cousin was named 'Cherub'. We loved our nan to death, we really did. Don't get me wrong, she still drank by the bottle, but she wasn't as wild as she once was. I can picture her house now. You walk in, living room on the left. Then you have the staircase on the left also, and then you walk into the kitchen ahead. Old creaky floorboard with the smell of ready salted crisps floating through the air. She loved those darn crisps. She always had a secret stash of Walkers crisps in the cupboard under her stairs, hidden in all her shopping bags. Then you'd have our grandad chomping away on his choc ices, those were his favorite also. You walk into their living room and there would be a bowl of mint humbug sweets, as well as a bowl of cheese savories. She loved her snacks, as do I. Maybe that's where I get it from. My nan was a sweetheart. She had such a heart of gold she did. But in a house of such love, there was such pain.

The Turn In The Road

My step-grandad was a dark and broken man. As a child, my dad never spoke much of him. My aunty never spoke much of him. Nor did my cousin speak much of him. It was always about our nan. We are going round to see nan, not nan AND step-grandad. It was like that growing up. So out of curiosity, I wanted to get to know my step-grandad. I would spend time with him, ask him questions and play games with him. And over a while, I grew attached to him. I looked up to him. He would take me down to the pub, buy me a diet coke, bag of crisps and play pool with me. He was still a drinker. He'd drink his ales and stouts. As he was Irish, he'd love a glass of Guinness. Because my mum's parents lived far away in the UK and my step mom's parents lived in South Africa, I grew close to my grandad. It soon turned into visiting my nan AND grandad for me because I liked how we got on. We would often watch a TV show called Eggheads, which was a quiz show. We'd watch it and get all the answers right, then make plans to go on the show ourselves because we could do it better than them. My grandad would give me money, let me sip his ale and do things that positioned him as the god-like figure in my life. Now we know that to be a form of grooming and manipulation. Because he would use his power and position to sexually molest me.

If you have been abused you'll know where I'm coming from when I say that I can't remember everything. I remember flashes. Which is exactly what trauma does to us. When we experience trauma, our brains go into survival mode and it tries it's very best to forget everything. Because with me, I can't remember how many times it happened and what happened specifically. But I can remember occasionally he would get me to sit on his lap whilst watching TV and he would slowly slide his hand down my pants and play with me. I can remember his heavy breathing in my ear, I can remember his erection pressing against me, I can remember looking up at him and he'll put his finger to his lips, soon followed by a "shhh" sound. Or he'd wink at me. There were times where he'd feel me up whilst I'm sitting on his lap, he'd stroke my hand whilst at the pub, he'd touch me up in random places of my nan's house. But here's the thing, sure I thought it was strange. I did think it was weird and there was a part of me that believed what he was doing was wrong. But then in the same light, I'm 10 years old and this is my grandad. He wouldn't be doing anything wrong to me because adults don't do wrong things, right? (which is what we believe when we are 10 years old).

I remember one night in particular. It was the first-ever time I was sleeping around overnight. My dad and stepmum were going out for a date night, as well as my aunt and her boyfriend at the time. So I stayed around my nans. As they were leaving I remember I was crying my eyes out on the couch in their living room, because I didn't want to stay around. Everyone just thought it was because I'd be bored. But truth be told, it was because I suddenly felt scared. I felt scared because I didn't know what more was going to happen with my grandad. Which

I admit was strange looking back because that means that deep down, I knew it was wrong. But his power over me forced me to keep quiet. That night my nan said that it was bedtime. So I head upstairs and get into bed in their spare bedroom. My nan and grandad are standing in the doorway. His arm around her waist. They both say goodnight to me and I say it back. But for the first time, I was looking at my grandad as a scared little boy. He's looking back at me, smiling. They turn the light out and pull the door to. I remember lying in bed, scared. I'm not a believer in god, but I was praying that he wasn't to come in. Because if he were to, where would it go? I didn't know what rape and sex really were back then. But I had a feeling there was more than just groping and fondling, and I was praying that I wouldn't find out. I was praying that he wouldn't come in and rape me. Looking back on it now, I have never been so scared and vulnerable in my entire life. A 10-year-old little boy who should be wanting to go to sleep so he can wake up and play with his friends. But instead, he wasn't able to sleep because he was scared that he'd be raped. Thankfully, he never came in that night. But something in me changed after that night. A small piece of me died. I wasn't the same kid anymore. My childhood from that point on had changed.

The Silence

A short while after we had a family gathering around my nan's house. There were a few of us there. My stepmum was sitting on the big couch whilst my grandad was on the single armchair facing the TV. He asked me onto his lap again, for which I did. At the time I didn't know why I did. I could have just made an excuse or gone into the kitchen. My family was there, so I was protected. But I still did it. That's because as a victim, you are powerless. You are controlled. No matter how much freedom you actually have (oftentimes you can just walk out of the door), you truly feel like you don't have any. It's like your body goes along with their spell whilst your mind is trying to pull you out.

As we were all watching TV, my grandad had his hand down my pants slowly massaging me. Notice how I mentioned people were in the same room? That's because I think he got a kick off that. It was a thrill. Anyway, my stepmum was on the other couch also watching TV. Out of the corner of her eye, she noticed my grandad drop his roll-up cigarette onto the floor. She takes no notice, assuming he was going to lean over and pick it up. But he doesn't. So she shifts her focus away from the TV and onto us. She noticed that his cigarette was now burning a hole in the carpet. She watched us and whilst she can't see any movement, her spidey-senses went off like crazy, causing her to walk out the room and call me into the kitchen. She told my dad, for which he questioned me about it on the way home. After some digging, I opened up about what he was doing.

Now, I don't remember any of that. That's a story of what happened from my stepmum, which is just another example of our brains shutting us off from certain memories. From that day on, I never went back to my nan's house. My dad didn't let me. He also told me to not tell anyone about what happened. He didn't want me to tell my friends or my school. Keep it at home. So I did. I never told a single person. I buried it deep down and tried to move on. For years I kept it quiet. But what I didn't know was the detrimental damage it was doing to my identity.

Each year I kept it quiet was another year where the shame and guilt grew. It was another year where I became more scared of someone finding out. It was another year where I got better at acting as someone else, wearing masks to protect the face underneath. I became so good at masking my emotions that no one would have ever guessed what was going on internally.

I remember when we as a family moved to a new location whilst I was at college. It was to a place where I knew no one. It was my chance to create an identity that I wanted people to see so that I could leave my old one behind. In London, I was shy, introverted, not confident, not great with the girls, and a virgin. All parts of me created by living in secrecy. But I remember seeing this new place being my chance to get out of my shell. So I went to this new college as someone who was super confident, a guy who had slept with loads of girls, he was extroverted and simply a great guy. Basically a complete lie at the time. But it worked. People believed it and more importantly, I soon believed it because the lie had started to become a truth. It became my escape which lasted a few years. I wore this new identity extremely well. Then one day, a guy that I follow online by the name of Lewis Howes had just released a book called 'The Mask Of Masculinity'. A book on how the average man wears masks to protect his vulnerabilities, in order to keep his image of masculinity intact. And BOOM... it hit me.

Growing up I looked to my dad on how to be a man. He was a proper 'man's man'. You'd very rarely see him cry. He asserted his dominance. He would do manly things. He had a bodybuilding and boxing background. I remember once when I got mugged by a guy in our local park. I went home crying and told my dad what happened. Seeing his reaction at the time inspired me to 'man up'. He turned all his rings round, grabbed the baseball bat, and told me to follow him. No other words were said. We walked through the park and I pointed out the group of people where he was originally hanging out. There must have been at least 10-12 of them. Without a second of hesitation, my dad was over there ready to beat on the kid, or all of them if it came to it. He used to tell me stories of when he was younger and in fights. So thinking he could take on a group of people wouldn't have surprised me. But the kid wasn't there. When we got back home, my dad said to me "you never, ever, let someone treat you or disrespect you like that again. You hear me?". I nodded, and I made a promise from that day that I never would.

So growing up, I very rarely cried. I tried to not think about the abuse because it would make me feel like I wasn't a man. I would never back down in an argument or fight, nor would I do things that I thought would come across as feminine. I would be the big-shot in front of guys, and the cocky asshole in front of the girls. But once I read The Mask Of Masculinity, I realized I had been hiding away behind multiple masks instead of showing my true self. I had been using this form of masculinity to further distance myself away from the story of my childhood. Then not too long after reading that book, a movie came out which completely changed everything for me - and it was a film called 'Spotlight'. It's a film about a team of journalists that uncover a story on child molestation charges against a local church in Boston, USA. If you haven't seen this yet, I highly recommend that you do. The film is crazy good. After watching it, my dad spoke to me about it in the car when he picked me up from the station:

"You've seen Spotlight, haven't you? Well, you know at the end of the film where they list all the locations, churches, and Catholic orphanages around the world with reported cases? Where your grandad grew up is listed there"

I couldn't believe it. My grandad was sexually abused as a child also? Is that what my dad was saying?

"Is that why he did it then?"

I remember my dad looked at me in shock when I asked that. As if I had attacked him.

"No. It's no reason for anything"

We arrived at the family home, he got out of the car and slammed the door. I just sat there, thinking, trying to make sense of everything. But I still couldn't wrap my head around it. My dad obviously knew more than he was letting on, otherwise, how did he know about grandad's school? Why was it a point he brought up? Why did it have meaning? I tried to ask my dad about it a few times after this but he never entertained the idea of it. He would either ignore the question or give me a one-worded answer.

Over the course of the next year, I actively worked on removing masks that I had grown so accustomed to wearing. I told my girlfriend at the time that the bad boy she fell for was a fake. I hadn't slept with all the girls as she once thought. It was all an act. I also told her about the abuse, completely preparing for her to walk away. But to my surprise, she didn't. She stayed and she supported me. She was a really good girl. I started to allow myself to feel my emotions when they came. So if that meant crying to the golden buzzer on Britain's Got Talent, then so be it (oh come on guys, it's emotional!). I grew sick and tired of being someone else. Of running away. Admittedly, I still couldn't tell anyone about the abuse (other than my girlfriend). I still believed that the world would outcast me. I believed people would either think I was lying or that I deserved it. That I was a sick child for letting my grandad sexually abuse me for over a year and do nothing about it. That was my belief and I honestly thought it wouldn't change. Then June 1st came around.

The Loss

I'm at home with my girlfriend and I receive two images from my little brother. One is an ambulance van outside the family home, and the other is of my dad lying on the bed with a paramedic standing next to him. In a panic, I call him up and my stepmum answers.

"What's going on mum?!"

"Hey, Perry. I don't want you to worry. They just need to take your dad down to the hospital to even out his blood sugar levels. That's all. They are going to take him down now, we are going to quickly finish our dinner and then we'll meet him down there to pick him up. I'll give you a call when we are back home."

Phew. Okay, false alarm. I put the phone down and carry on with what I was doing at the time. An hour later my girlfriend and I are sitting on the couch watching TV. My phone rings and it's my little brother.

"Hey Trav, you guys back home yeah?"

"No. Dad's gone."

"Huh?"

"Dad's gone."

"What do you mean gone? Gone where?"

"He's dead. He's gone. He had a heart attack in the ambulance van. He didn't make it to the hospital."

And it was in that exact moment everything came crashing down. I remember sliding off the couch, screaming in shock and horror. My girlfriend took the phone out of my hand and rushed out into the garden. I sat there trying to register what had just happened and I couldn't bring myself to believe it. After a while, she came back in and just looked at me. I shook my head in disbelief.

"No. That didn't just happen. It's a sick joke. He's still alive."

My girlfriend didn't know what to say to me. We waited for her dad to come and get us. I got into the back of the car and stared out the window. It was the longest car journey in the world, or though it seemed. Because the world just slowed down. My cousin called me up, crying.

"Perry, is it true? Is Uncle A dead?"

"No, it's not. It's just a sick joke. Watch when I get there, he'll be alive and breathing."

I truly believed it was a joke. I absolutely refused to believe that my dad had just died. I remember pulling up outside the hospital, my grandma (this is my stepmom's mum from South Africa) was standing outside, crying. She hugged me and I walked inside. Family and friends were there waiting for me to arrive before seeing his body. The doctor draws the curtain back and there he was, laying on the hospital bed. His mouth was open as if he was snoring and his skin had already changed colour. It was the most surreal image I'd ever seen. Then the reality came crashing down and I was in pieces. I had just lost not only my dad but also my best friend. A type of harsh reality you never thought you'd have to get used to, especially in your early 20s.

The following months were some of the hardest I'd ever encountered. Losing a parent is something you see in the movies, it's hard to truly connect to it. But then when it happens to you, it's very surreal. I can never explain to someone what it's like to lose a parent, especially a parent who you had planned to be around for much longer (he was 48 when he passed away). Even today I don't know how I deal with it, every day is different. However, like with most things, it gets better with time.

But there was one day, one morning to be specific, I was brushing my teeth. I spit the toothpaste out and catch myself in the mirror. I just looked. I looked at myself. I looked at where I've been, where I was going and what changes I needed to make. Whilst I had done a lot of work to remove my masks and detach myself from the notion I had around masculinity, I knew there was still more to do. I did not want to drop dead from a sudden heart attack before the age of 50 and leave behind a family. That was not an option for me. But I knew if I didn't own the story of my childhood, if I didn't speak up and break my silence, I could very well go down the same path as my dad. Because I knew he was hiding a part of himself. I knew he was living in secrecy. But I just didn't know what it was.

Breaking The Silence

Not too long after I was at a business mastermind retreat. There were me and 4 other business owners there and it was day one of the event. The hosts asked us to open up and share with the group our story. It started on the other side of the room, meaning I was the last one to speak as I was on the opposite side. And whilst people were sharing, one by one, all I could think about was sharing my story on sexual abuse. But the voices kicked in telling me not to do it.

"Why do you want to do that? That's too much personal information. Nobody wants to know. They don't care. To be honest, if you did tell them, they'll look at you differently. They won't talk to you at lunch. You'll just make it awkward for everyone."

That's what the voices were saying in my head. I could hear it loud and clear. Then before I knew it, it was my turn. I remember there being a brief silence. They were looking at me to talk, probably wondering why I hadn't started saying anything yet. And that was because I was busy fighting off that voice. If I didn't share my story right there and then, I never would. So I open my mouth and just start talking without putting any thought into it. There was no filter. It was just word vomit. I can't remember everything I said because it was 14 years worth of silence being broken within 60 seconds. I just looked at the floor and spoke. Then once I shared my story, I could feel the silence. In the break, one of the business owners came over to me and thanked me for sharing. She told me how brave I was. How me opening up allowed space for the group to come together as one. She also said that I was an inspiration.

This was a reaction I never thought I'd experience off the back-end of sharing my story. Which is why on the drive home two days later, I needed to share it again. Because I knew that once I got home and settled back into the life I was living before the mastermind event, I may never talk about it again. Which I didn't want to happen. So I pulled my car over into a side-road and turned the engine off. I took my phone out and placed it into the holder on my dashboard. I hit record. I start talking about the abuse. My nerves kick in, the negative voices kick in, and I turn the video off. I put my seatbelt back on and was about to turn the engine back on, but I knew I couldn't let my silence keep me pinned down. So I tried again. I start crying and then turn the video off again. I didn't want people to see me cry because they'll think I'm weak and pathetic. Then I quickly realised that was a mask I had worked so hard on getting rid of, there was no time to allow it to creep back in. So I hit record again. It took me 7 takes to get this 20-minute video recorded and uploaded to Facebook. I talk about my childhood sexual abuse, my dad's death and the struggles in detail. Once I uploaded it to Facebook, I put my phone down and closed my eyes. I'm thinking of all the bad things that are going to happen from doing this. The unfriends, the horrible messages, the hate, the shaming and the bullying. A couple of minutes went by and I looked at my phone,

60 people had viewed it but only 2 people had left a comment. So in my mind right there, 58 people had watched it and thought bad things about me. I was about to delete it, but I stopped myself. I then realised something that became powerful, and it was the fact that the video wasn't for anyone else, it was for me. I was sharing my story and breaking my silence for me! Because I grew too tired of living in darkness. I grew tired of thinking I was different, a freak, and that I was broken. I needed to shed that part of myself and show the person in the mirror that I'm not those things. So I threw my phone into the back of the car (so I couldn't reach it whilst driving) and drove home. Once home, I lean back and grab my phone. My heart sinks as I click the unlock button. But to my surprise, there I see it, a ton of notifications and messages from people. Every single one was words of encouragement, support and love. Each message was the same, including one of them being how I helped pull him out of a dark place as he was going through something similar. Whilst reading through all of this, I just started to cry. Because I realised that the world wasn't as dark as I thought it was. It was actually very bright and beautiful, I had just chosen not to see that. The external world I had been seeing was just in fact a reflection of my internal world.

A short while after the beautiful response I had gotten, I had realised there was still work to do. There was still healing that needed to be done. Because after 14 years, I had finally allowed myself to fully explore what happened in my childhood. There was still shame, guilt and resentment towards my grandad and I. So I asked a friend what he thought should be the next step. This was a friend who lost his dad and did a lot of work on himself to get through it. After a call with him, I left knowing exactly what I needed to find. Now, don't get me wrong. I knew what I needed to find, but I didn't have the steps on how to actually get there. That was my job to figure out. And that place was total forgiveness. Forgiveness towards myself, towards my dad, and my grandad.

It's interesting because growing up, we all know what forgiveness is. The type of thing where your brother accidentally breaks your toy, so your mum asks you to forgive and forget. You know, that type of forgiveness. But when in truth, forgiveness has tremendous power if we allow ourselves to use it effectively. When it came to my dad's death, I blamed him for so much. I blamed him for smothering me growing up. I blamed him for asking me to fill up his vodka bottle with water so my stepmom wouldn't find out. I blamed him for becoming spiteful and immature towards me. Then the last 3 years of his life, I blamed him for becoming an alcoholic, for being negative, and for dying. I blamed him for being selfish and leaving us behind. Then I blamed myself for blaming him. I blamed myself for not telling my stepmum about his alcohol problems, I blamed myself for all the times I would ignore my dad's calls because I knew he was looking for an argument. Blame blame blame. And the thing is, when we hold onto blame, it's impossible to move forward. Blame is tied to the past, and we can't move forward if we are tied to the past. So I worked on forgiving myself and forgiving my dad. Once I did that, it was time to work on my childhood. It was time to forgive myself for not speaking out. It was time to forgive myself for letting it happen. Then it was time to forgive my grandad.

Here's the thing, I always get comments from people saying

"you forgave your grandad? How could you?!", and if you're thinking that, then I understand why. But here is what I want you to understand. Forgiving your abuser is not giving them a Get Out Of Jail Free card. It does not excuse them for what they did to you. It doesn't let them off the hook. You are forgiving them because you are too special, worthy and beautiful of a human being to let this person have control over you. Because if you can't forgive them, then you are still tied to them. You are attached. You need to detach yourself. There is immense power in detachment because once you detach, you gain control. You now have the power. Buddha once said *"The root of suffering is attachment"*, and he's not wrong.

I speak a lot about identity shifts. You have the identity you are today, which is one that is still hurt, suffering and attached to your past story. And you have the future identity of you, the one that you envision yourself being. The sooner you can become aware that the identity you have today is now your OLD identity, you are one step closer to stepping into the shoes of your new identity. It's a powerful realisation once we understand there is a choice. There is always a choice, and we have the power to choose. Just like forgiveness. We have the power to choose to forgive that person. There's no argument in the fact that it will probably be the hardest thing you'll ever have to do. But it's either staying hurt and in resentment or allowing yourself to move forward feeling free. Which one would you choose?

The Lightbulb Moment

Once I had shared my story a few times online, I visited my aunt in London (the first time since sharing my story publicly). I was sitting in the living room with my aunt and cousin, drinking a coffee, and we got onto the topic of my abuse. I found out that everyone in my family who knew about what happened to me thought it only occurred that one time when my stepmum called me into the kitchen. Which I wasn't actually aware of. I assumed that when my dad questioned me as a kid, I would have mentioned all the other times. But I guess even at that moment I was too scared to mention it.

They then proceeded to tell me that I wasn't the only one who had been abused by him. There are 3 other members of the family that were also victims, my cousin being one, and my dad is another. Which completely blew my mind. I knew of my cousin being a victim, but not my dad.

My aunt went on to then say that my step-grandad grew up in a Catholic Church in Ireland, along with his brother, where there were multiple cases of sexual abuse. When my step-grandad's sisters questioned him about what happened at the school, his only response was *"I did what I had to do to protect my brother."*

As soon as I found this out, everything clicked into place.

There was a reason my dad told me to keep silent. There was a reason he became an alcoholic. My dad never knew how to deal with his story. He lived his whole life in shame, guilt, and anger. He resented my grandad for what he did, but he also had an extreme amount of guilt once he found out I had also been abused by him. Bessel Van Der Kolk, one of the world's leading experts on traumatic stress, says *"People cannot put traumatic events behind them until they are able to acknowledge what has happened and start to recognize the invisible demons they're struggling with"*. He said that in his book called 'The Body Keeps The Score', which I highly recommend you read. My dad was constantly running away from his past. His coping mechanism was alcohol. Over time his stress levels went through the roof. He had alarmingly high blood pressure. He became a diabetic and died from a heart attack 5 months later. It was a long downhill battle. Going back to what Bessel mentioned, if we can not confront the demons in our past, we are fighting a losing battle. I remember a few weeks before his death my dad popped over to my house. He was drunk and spoke about the argument he just had with my stepmum. After venting, he left and I texted him later on that day and asked him why he was drinking so much. Do you know what he replied with? Just one sentence, *"To fight away the demons."*

My dad struggled, and it breaks my heart knowing he was in so much pain. My stepmum sent him to AA meetings, but that didn't last long before my dad stopped going. Probably because attending them was admitting to himself he had a problem, and my dad wasn't one for admitting that. As for my step-grandad, I felt sorry for him also. It's evident he was abused by those priests, perhaps along with his brother, for a considerable amount of time and he struggled with the story in the same way my dad had. But whereas my dad took the path of self-infliction to cope, my step-grandad took the path of inflicting his pain onto other people to cope. Knowing his story enabled me to find the path of forgiveness much quicker. It made me realize that no one is born a child molester. Nine times out of ten, the certain individual went through certain events that altered their way of thinking, their behavior, and identity, to put them onto the path of hurting other people in the same way. I'm not for a second excusing their behavior. I'm simply stepping out of the emotional shoes so I can see, think and feel more clearly. From a place of understanding, so I can arrive at true forgiveness quicker. The quicker I am there, the quicker I can move on.

I'm also not suggesting that once you find forgiveness you will be able to move on. That might not be the case for you which is why I strongly suggest seeking out a professional therapist to help you through this. However, it's a great place to start. For me, finding forgiveness worked. Diving into my step-grandad's story and creating awareness worked. If he was alive today, I would sit down with him. I would like to talk to him and see if I could get him to open up and share his story. I probably would have included his story inside this book. Because I believe that every damaged soul can be saved to some degree.

My Purpose

From this moment on, I wanted to help as many survivors as I could to break their silence. I knew there were countless Perrys out there struggling in silence. I wanted to do everything I could to stop the silent suffering and early deaths of people just like my dad. So I ramped up my social media content and spoke a lot about my story, sexual abuse and breaking the silence of suffering. I took to TikTok because it was a relatively new platform at the time. It was mainly used by kids and teenagers to dance and sing on. But I knew that as unfortunate as it was, the audience that uses this app are the ones who need to hear my message most because they are the ones going through it. So I created countless videos covering my story, my dad's story and other inspirational videos to give these kids a voice to listen to. Very quickly I started to pick up traction. I gained over 100,000 followers in less than 2 months and had new people messaging me every day on Instagram sharing their story with me. But very quickly I hit a roadblock. I felt like an impostor. I felt like all these people were looking to me for a magic cure. Or like I am a therapist that could help them. The messages were piling in and my responses stopped. I couldn't bear to read another message from a girl who was being raped by her dad or being abused by her brother or her uncle. I didn't know what I could say back that would heal them. I didn't know what I could say that would take away their pain. It was quite a surreal experience. However, after a couple of weeks, I was in meditation and I realised something that changed everything. It led me to reply to every single message and brought me to this point right here, writing this book for you. And it's this...

People weren't looking to me for the cure!

How do I know? Because when I look back in my story, back to when I was in silence, I just wanted to share it without judgment. I just wanted someone who would listen. Someone who was there.

Because living in silence makes you feel lonely. Even though there are countless people all around you, all who very much love you, you still feel alone. And because you are alone with this secret side to you, you can't help but judge yourself. You can't help but feel ashamed and scared of that piece of you. So when you look out there into the world, you assume that the world would think the same thing and feel the same way about you. Which leads me back to a point I was saying earlier on, that the external world is just a reflection of your internal world.

So when it comes to sharing our story, we feel like we can't. We feel like we aren't allowed to. For this exact reason is why I share my story and urge others to do the same. Because once we share our story, we give those who relate the permission to do the same. Us survivors just want to be heard. We have kept hidden away in the dark for so long that we just want to be seen. That is our 'cure' if you want to call it that. So when I realised this, I wanted to give as many sexually abused victims as I could the permission, power and platform to share their story. So they can also break their silence and be heard. This book is about exactly that. It's about you breaking your silence. It's about owning your story. It's about reading the stories inside this book and realising that you aren't alone. That there are plenty of people out there who can relate to you, who do love you, who do see you, who do hear you, and who are there for you.

II

Part 2. Stories From Survivors Of Sexual Abuse

You will be reading the stories of others who have been through abuse. If you get triggered whilst reading any of these stories, you can skip it. So don't feel like you have to put yourself through anything that you do not want to experience. It's completely your choice. At the same time, you may find connection and inspiration from reading through these stories. It may be one story you read that empowers you to break your silence. Whatever you do, you got this. You are strong.

Kellie Kavanagh

Sometime after my conversation with my aunt and cousin, my cousin spoke to me about wanting to bravely share her story one day. She asked me what the best way I thought was, for which I replied saying that there was no best way. After some thought, she said she wanted to do a video with me to go onto Facebook. I was so proud of her because it's such a huge first step for someone who hasn't spoken out about it further than their own family. So one weekend I went over, made sure she was still okay to do it, and I sat with her. What you are about to read next is the text transcription of the video we did together. I have not edited any of this out of respect to the authenticity and vulnerability that she showed.

This is my cousin breaking her silence, publicly for the first time, on her story of sexual abuse. The effect it had on her, and how she deals with it today.

"Hi guys. I'm Kellie. I'm 30 years of age. Aquarius. Born and raised in Acton, West London. I grew up a normal, happy child. In a sense of my mum. My mum, she is my rock. She's done everything she possibly can for me, as a single parent. Because I was also brought

up in a broken home. My mum and dad, well, my mum broke up with my dad because my dad cheated and it just didn't work out between them. That was before I was the age of 1 I think. So yeah, for over 29 years she's raised me as a single parent. He went on to have my brother and my beautiful sister. Who both of them I think I've only ever met once. Which is very heartbreaking because we might not have the same mums but we're still blood. But yeah. Even though I grew up happy, I had friends and I thought I was happy, but there was just things going on that nobody knew about. And um, I kinda kept to myself. So, um... ah fuck."

It was at this moment my cousin's mind kicked in and the defence walls went straight up, trying to talk her out of it. She started to cry. But after a deep breath, she persevered.

"I'm guessing a lot of you have heard Perry's story about our step-grandad. He played a big part in my life, personally. Not for the right reasons. I wish my nan had never met him. Bless her soul. So for those of you who have heard Perry's story, you'll know what he went through. And obviously he wasn't the only family member that went through that. So, I'm going to personally speak of what happened to me. From as far as I can remember it was sexual abuse, to put it bluntly. I remember he used to make me go in the garden and urm... from the garden to inside the house there was a bit where they had an outside toilet. It was quite an old fashioned house. So they had an outside toilet. And every time I went to use the toilet if my mum wasn't there, he would come and open the door. There was a game he used to like to play where he used to put things in his clothes and would make me find them. So like a hide and seek with balls. Bouncy balls. Basically just copping a feel and just doing things he shouldn't, nobody should be doing. To a child. To anybody.

And he used to tell me that it was normal. And the times that I did use to question it, he used to tell me that no one would believe it anyway. They would say I'm lying. I'm just doing it for attention. So I didn't even tell my mum. And obviously I knew my mum would protect me, I knew my mum would help me, I knew my mum would do something about it. But he made me feel like it was normal. And it wasn't until your friends went on 6 weeks holidays and that, and they came back and you ask them what they did. They've gone on holiday with their grandparents and you ask them how their grandparents are with them, especially their grandad because that's the role he was meant to play. And it was completely different to what I was experiencing. That's when I started realising that it wasn't normal. It wasn't normal for your step-grandad to put their hands down your trousers and make you touch their private parts, and touch you in places with their private parts that they shouldn't be doing. And it took me a long time to realise that what he was doing was wrong because of what he used to say to me. And then once I got... I think it basically stopped when I was probably about 12/13. And was probably going on for as young as I can remember. And it was probably every other Sunday when we used to go there. So I was very good at hiding it. From my mum obviously, and from the rest of my family. Because I think if people had found out, he would have been dead and people would have been in jail, let's put it that way. But once I did tell my mum, he was confronted. And he denied the whole thing. He said that I was just doing it for attention. My mum believed me. Of course, she believed me. So from then, I didn't really go around to see my nan as much. My relationship with my nan started crumbling. Because of him. Because of that. Then he passed away, he died from a heart attack. Karmas a bitch. Then after that my nan started deteriorating, and we lost my nan. So I feel like he stole a lot from me. He stole my innocence. He stole my nan because she wasn't the same. I think she wasn't happy, she wasn't happily married. She was drunk a lot. My family seems to do that a lot, they turn to alcohol. Which is something I kinda grew out of. And I learned to not rely on alcohol because I learned it doesn't cure the problem. So that was basically from primary school to throughout high school. Well, until I was about 12/13. And then once that had kinda set aside, and he was gone, and I didn't have that problem anymore, I didn't have the worry of this man doing whatever he was doing to me... so I started in high school and I think it was in year 8, that's when the problems started. It was just the odd name-calling and things like that. Nothing major. But then it started getting worse. And it was a lot too, it like, it knocks your confidence. It makes you feel depressed. You start to feel a way about yourself. You start to feel like you have to do this to yourself, and you have to look this way and you have to do this to fit in. And then the bullying started getting worse. To the point where I was being verbally attacked in school to literally having people waiting outside the front gates for me. I can't really explain why. I can't really explain, I can't say "oh yeah they were doing this because of this reason". I know one reason was because I supposedly slept with somebody and then it all came out that it wasn't me. It was actually someone I was friends with at the time.So they kicked my head in for no reason. The bullying got so bad that I started bunking school. I basically fucked my education up due to it. Fucked my GCSEs, fucked up everything. Due to not wanting to go to school because I was being bullied. Then my mum got threatened, they said that my mum would go to jail if I didn't start going to school. Regardless of the fact that I was being bullied, they didn't give a fuck about that. This is the same school that I had also told what my grandad had been doing to me, and they didn't get anybody involved or anything until he died. That's when they wanted to pay attention. So I agreed to go to school. But instead of allowing me to go back to my classes, I got put in a block with the naughty kids called 'modified curriculum'. I got put in with the naughty kids because I was bunking. But I was bunking because I was being bullied. I'm not a vicious person, but everyone has their points. I wish looking back that one of the times a girl came up to me and punched me, that I just hit them straight back. All the times my mum used to tell me to hit back, I should have listened and hit them back. Maybe the bullying would have stopped. But I didn't listen, I was too scared. And maybe that stems from my step-grandad. I just felt like I was worthless. Like I deserved it maybe. It got to the point where one of the girls actually wore her friend's school uniform, she didn't go to the school, but she wore her friend's school uniform, and she came into the school looking for me. That didn't phase the teachers. Until one day when I was walking home from school and I saw two of them. Two of these girls that were part of the group. And they took me down a road and within a couple of minutes I saw the other two around the corner. And I don't know for about, it felt like forever, but it was probably about 10 minutes, they punched me, they kicked me, they stamped on my head, they threw my head against the wall, they threw me against the car. They pulled a lot of my hair out. I had scratches all down my back. To be fair I only had a couple of bumps on my head, considering what they did. But obviously, that was just on the outside. Nobody knew what they had done on the inside. And funnily enough a lot of people stood there and watched what these girls had done. It took for a stranger to pull up in his car, drag the girls off me and told me to get into the car. It was either get in the car with this random man or continue to get beat up. So I got in the car. He drove me straight to the police and my parents, well, my mum and her boyfriend at the time came to get me. Which then brings me to the next part of my life. A few months later after that incident happened and I had left school, I was just chilling with one of my friends at the time. I think I was very depressed at this stage. I actually took a bottle of my mum's Baileys or something. Some alcohol. And went to a park and got completely drunk off my head. Went back to her house and threw up everywhere. That's when I realised alcohol is not the solution. So by this point, I had already started smoking. I started smoking weed. And to be fair in the beginning, I only smoked it so I could block everything out. But then obviously over time, it becomes a habit. I used that more and I laid off the alcohol. Now a week or two after this, we went to one of her friend's birthday parties. We went and got some weed off someone, went to the park, rolled it, started smoking it, felt fine. Got to her friend's house and as I reached the door I started feeling funny. I didn't know what was wrong with me, I just knew I needed to sit down. My legs felt weak, everything just felt funny. So I went and sat down on the wall, but across the road. Now she was talking to her friend saying happy birthday, and apparently the next thing she saw was me on the floor with my head in between my legs. Shaking. They all ran over, tried to lay me down, and when I came round they sat me up on the wall. And then told me what had happened. And I was like "what? What the fuck you talking about?". Now across the road, and it happened again. But I had just collapsed on the floor. One of the boys there picked me up, bless him. He started carrying me into the house. And as he went to take me up the first flight of stairs, I started shaking again. So he put me down on the floor. And then I stopped. So he picked me up again and started taking me back up the stairs. I started shaking again. This occurred inside the house 3 or 4 times. So all in all, I had about 5 or 6 seizures, which I later came to realise. The girl's mum asked me if I wanted an ambulance, I said no because I thought I had taken funny weed. I thought it was the weed. But I went back to the source and found out that it wasn't. So I just left it. I didn't bother. Months went on and it happened again. It wasn't until I told my mum and my mum actually saw it happen, that she called an ambulance. And we found out that I was having multiple seizures. And they were the type of seizures where your whole body shuts down. Sometimes you wet yourself. You froth at the mouth. You bite your tongue. Not something I would wish on my worst enemy. Even these girls that previously kicked the shit out of me, I wouldn't even wish it on them. So they started putting me on medication. Different trials, nothing was working. But the seizures would come and go. So I would be okay for a few months, or even a year, and then the next year would be a year full of seizures. It just depended. Then they did a brain scan because they didn't understand why at the age of 16, I had just started having seizures. So they did a brain scan. And it turns out that I had an AVM on my brain. Now an AVM, I've written it down so I could say it properly. Now an AVM stands for Arteriovenous Malformation. It's basically a tangle of the abnormal blood vessels. Arteries and veins and things like that. They describe it as like a birthmark on the brain. This is on my left side. And it's right here. They have a higher risk of bleeding than normal blood vessels in your head. And when they bleed out properly, they can cause a haemorrhage, which leads to stroke, death. Now when they found this out, they realised that it had been ruptured, and that was the cause of the seizures. Because the AVM has been there since birth, it doesn't just happen. And they asked questions like "have you knocked your head?" blah blah blah. And you just say no no no because that was probably the cause of it. Obviously it might not be, but I didn't have seizures before that. It didn't rupture before that. But now all of a sudden, after all of this has happened, it's ruptured. And it's bleeding. And because I was young, they didn't want to do proper surgery because I hadn't had kids yet. So they did something called a 'gamma knife' treatment, where I had to have a thing bolted and screwed into my head, and have lasers going to the AVM to try and shrink it, so it was less dangerous for me. And it didn't work. I got lost in the hospital system. So for a couple of years, I also fell pregnant, and it wasn't until I fell pregnant after however many years of being lost on the system, that I was finally put back onto their system. Because obviously you have to go to the hospital when you're pregnant. Had my son. He's now 5. And they've basically waited all this time saying there was nothing they could do, so I just got on with my life and prayed that this thing in my head doesn't bleed out even more. Then I get told that they can do a surgery. And they can glue around it, which would stop the blood from getting to the rest of my brain. So it would basically stop it from killing me. So I thought, "Great. You know. Woohoo". Then I was told that having this surgery would, basically to go into this surgery, I need to come to terms that I would most likely come out of it with loss of vision in my right eye. So I would only have sight in my left eye. And if I do have sight in my right eye, it won't be that much. If I don't lose my sight in my right eye, it's a blessing. Which is something that is not easy to take in. How do you come to terms with that? Then they say that with any operational surgery, that there is a chance of stroke and there is a chance of death. Now what also comes along, I went for an appointment on Tuesday because my surgery is tomorrow. And it's two surgeries in one. So the first surgery is going to be an angiogram, through the groin. Which they put the tube through to your brain and they try and glue around it. Now the second surgery, that's the one that scares me. Not only are they going to cut my hair, they are going to shave my hair. Yeah, as girls know, we like our hair. They're going to shave a horseshoe like this, in my head. So they can cut through to the skull and get to the AVM, so they can remove what's left over from them trying to glue it. But in doing that can create so many side-effects. That is the surgery that will create the loss of vision, it can create memory loss, worse case scenario is stroke and death. It's hard. It's hard to grasp. It's hard to come to terms with. It's hard to look at your mum and just say that everything is going to be fine. Or talk about it with your partner and expect them to not feel a way. Or look at your son, knowing that in a couple of days you are going into hospital and even though you are praying for the best outcome, anything can happen. Knowing that you are not going to see your child for however many days. Possibly, if you're ever going to see them again. It's hard to try and completely stay positive. When people say to stay positive, it's easier said than done. I am praying and hoping for the best. But it's hard. People will see me on the street, or they'll see my pictures on Facebook and they'll be like "Oh, she looks so happy". And it's like, I am happy with what I have. And it's taken me a long time to realise that. But, I'm not rich. I have money problems. I don't have flashy clothes. I don't have the best of everything. You know, I try to give that to my son. And I'm grateful. Yeah, I might bitch and moan. Yeah, I might look like shit sometimes. But I like seeing my son smile. And seeing my family smile and be happy. That's a thing I regret, with my uncle. And losing my uncle. I wish I had spent more time with him once he moved out of London. Because I'll never get that time back. None of us will. And that's still something I haven't come to terms with. And his death was also a big slap in the face. Which is obviously Perry's dad. It was a massive shock to my system. I wish I did spend more time with him, I did phone more and I did text more. Because I can't now. I can't get the big bear hugs anymore. I can't get the "oh shut up you silly idiot" anymore. The "cheer up, stop being so stroppy". I think his death was a big wake up call for me when it comes to simple blessings. Always creating memories. The simple things in life that you should be enjoying and making the most of. Not everyday is going to be happy, but just making the most out of every day you possibly can and the people around you. Because you don't know what's going to happen in life. I didn't know when I was younger that my step-grandad was going to do all these things to me. I didn't know that once I got into highschool I was going to start being bullied, to the point where it completely changed me as a person. I didn't know that, that many knocks to the head would create this condition that I didn't even know I had, and made it worse. Which I am now suffering for. I had seizures whilst I was pregnant with my child, and I have to give thanks that no harm came to him. And now at the age he is, he has to see me have seizures. He sees me have seizures and goes to tell my mum if it's only my mum that's here. He then waits and asks me if I'm okay and gives me a kiss. He's 5. As much as it's nice for him to do that, I don't want my child seeing me like that. No parent wants their child seeing them that way. I don't know, this is just an insight into my life and my story. I could come out of this surgery and I could be okay. Or I could come out of it with eye loss and try to adapt to that. Which I don't know how I'm going to do because I also started a hairdressing course, which I never thought would happen. Because of the simple fact that I had this condition and had been told that I was a liability by other workplaces. So I thought "No, I'm never going to get the chance to do this". This is something I've wanted to do since I was young. But it's not going to happen, I'm too old now. And this condition is going to get in the way. And even though I told them about my condition, they gave me the chance. They were like "Why can't you be a hairdresser? Why can't you fulfil your dreams? Why can't you do what you want to do with your life?". And for that I'll forever be grateful for them. Because they showed me that I, that I can. They showed me that I have that ability, they brought it out of me. Because obviously it's always been there. But they helped to bring that out. And on this course I've met some amazing people. I struggle to meet people due to my condition. I find it hard to talk to people and to communicate because I do go brain-dead a lot."

Feeling a slight pause in my cousin sharing her story, I wanted to ask a question based on confidence. More importantly, how she found the confidence within herself to pursue the hairdressing course.

"Can I ask a question? So you've had jobs before where you've had seizures, and it's affected you. What made you have the confidence to pursue this hairdressing course knowing that you may have seizures on the job again and that it may affect you even more? What made you go forward with it?"

"Urm, because I was actually forced to go to a job fair by the jobcentre." She proceeded to say, "There was a lady there and it was hairdressing. I thought "oh, let me check it out". But nothing came of it. Then I was asked to go to another job fair and they were there again. And I thought to myself, "you know what, this is a sign. I know it sounds stupid. But this is a sign, so let me just take the chance". I was upfront with them. I told them all about my condition. I told them I had been called a liability by other hairdressing courses. And she was just like "no. We'll sign you up. You can come in, come for an interview". I had to do a couple of tests and that was it. They gave me the chance. And I'm so thankful for that. I let my condition get in the way for so many years, that I thought it was either now or never. And I love it. And luckily enough I've been given the chance whilst I'm having the surgery, whilst I'm having to recover, for the time to recover. They are giving me the time and allowing me to go

back in my own time. And now with my surgery in the morning, I have my cousins down to stay with me for support. And also to do this video. I hope that sharing my story does help people. I don't really open up properly to people. They kinda know bits. But this is the most I have ever opened up, publicly. Especially about my step-grandad. Which is something very, very hard."

I go on to ask her how she now feels after sharing her story.

"I feel better. But now that I have got it out, it's out. It'll take a couple of days for me to, you know... but it's out there. And after pressing the stop button on this video, I may regret some of the things that I have said. But fuck it. It's my story. If they don't like it, they don't like it. But hopefully, it helps somebody else because there are people who might not have gone through what I have gone through, there are people who might have gone through similar bits. Or know someone who has."

To tie it up, I ask one last question...

"For those who have been through something similar, what would you think you could say to them to maybe help get them through it?"

"Talk to people. Talk to people. Because I hold it in. I hold a lot of my stuff in. And, as much as people don't see it, I have a lot of anger in me. I think once I recover I should join a boxing club or something, just to let out that steam" We both laugh. "But um, definitely talk to people. Talk about it. And for people who suffer with seizures, find a group who specialise in that. People who you can relate to, and all talk about it. Because I didn't do that and I think I should have. I

think I should have spoken out about my step-grandad. Or kicked him in the balls. You know? Just done something. But it's done. You can't go back. But right now, you have to speak to someone. There will always be someone out there who is willing to listen to you and who is willing to help you. Regardless."

I know this was super hard for my cousin to share, and going through her story highlights a few areas that a lot of survivors face. One of them being the need for approval. The urge to fit in. That was me once upon a time. Lying in my nan's spare bed alone and scared, that was the moment all of my self-confidence and my self-worth was stripped away. My self-image was shattered. I felt different around my friends. I felt alone and ashamed. My external world completely changed. Maybe you feel the same way too. Maybe you feel like you wake up every day with the intention set on blending in. Your lack of confidence prevents you from showing up as the most powerful version of yourself. And if that is you, that's okay. Don't be hard on yourself. By the time you finish reading this book, I'm hoping you'll be able to see yourself differently. You'll be able to treat yourself with love, kindness and find forgiveness so you can move on with your life. Moving forward as the most powerful version of yourself, completely detached from the negative chapters in your past.

Alisha Gee

Sometime later after my cousin shared her story, I got introduced to someone who was also a survivor of sexual abuse. An incredibly brave soul who used fitness as her way of fighting through pain and struggles. I was a fitness coach for nearly 4 years, so I know just how important health and fitness can be for someone who is going through a rough patch. Fitness can be an escape. It can be a coping mechanism. It can be a lifeline. Intrigued to know what her story was, I asked if she was willing to share it with me, for which she kindly accepted. Below is Alisha Gee sharing her story.

"It started with confusion. My abuser would always tell me that it was normal. But every time he touched me, I knew it wasn't okay. And so it went on to make me feel ashamed of what had been going on. The guilt for wondering why I didn't stop it in the beginning, and why I just couldn't go and get help. I was so scared though that my abuser was right. And that everyone would just think that it was my fault. Those fears became reality. My mum came to me and she told me that she knew what had been going on and that she wanted to hear my side of the story. And I remember this like it was yesterday. I was spinning around in my office chair, telling her briefly what I could get out of my mouth about the past. She looked at me and

said, "Alisha, it takes two". And that reaffirmed that it was my fault. And I know now that 39% of women also experience some kind of fear of telling somebody because they won't be believed. Which leads to even more self-destruction. Which was true in my own life. Because in high school, in college, I used things like men, drinking and partying to mask how I was feeling. I used to feel so guilty and shameful about those actions, and those coping mechanisms. Because that wasn't me. But what I realised now was to forgive myself. Because I was fighting for myself the only way I knew how. After college, I was so lost and confused at what I wanted to even do with my life. So I ended up working at a home for girls who had gone through sex trafficking. I felt so connected to these girls because they had gone through abuse as well. And had low self-esteem. And didn't feel heard. Or seen. Which ultimately lead them into the hands of sex traffickers. That is when someone close to me came to me, my boyfriend Eric came to me and said, "Alisha, I know you love these girls. But you have never even helped yourself. How can you help yourself?". And that's when I realised that enough is enough. No matter how painful it was to look back at my past, I needed to change my life. So the first step for me was forgiving the people that hurt me the most. And then I looked at what it was that I actually loved to do. And to find out who I was, and what made me happy. So for two years I worked on myself, focused on myself. Through coaches, reading books, through fitness... and that's when I realised that's why I went through abuse. To become the person that I am today. Fitness has been the number one way of fighting for myself after the abuse. It told my mind that I was not broken anymore. It helped me to start loving my body again."

The fear of being blamed and not believed is something that many survivors face. This may be the biggest worry for you. If it is, I can understand. Because the harsh reality is that just like Alisha, you may tell someone and they could throw it back in your face. And it could leave you in a worse place than before you even told them. Which is why you have to detach yourself from their reaction. The second you plan to share your story with someone but hope for a specific reaction from them, you are putting yourself on the line. Their reaction is completely out of your control. Therefore you should only be sharing your story for you. Not to prove a point. Not to claim your innocence. No, simply sharing it to break the silence you have been trapped in for so long. To reclaim your power. To fight back. For you! No one else. When I was uploading my story to Facebook, I didn't do it for a specific reaction. Sure I was scared and nervous. But I was doing it for me, and me only. Just to add, if someone does have a negative reaction to your story, there is no telling where they are in their story. They could have gone through abuse. They could be living in silence and currently fighting off their own demons. So try not to let their negativity undo the amazing and courageous act you had just done by breaking your silence.

Lastly, Alisha touched upon something so important when she spoke about finding what made her happy. Your happiness is the most important thing in the entire world, it truly is. I ask myself every day (I also ask those closest to me), "Are you happy?". If the answer is yes, then that's all that matters. If the answer is no, then changing it to a yes needs to be at the top of your priority list. Go and paint. Sing. Run. Do whatever makes your inner-child beam with happiness. Then let that happiness ripple out into the external world.

Vlad Negrau

This story is a powerful one for different reasons. Ever since I opened up about my abuse, I thought I would see other men open up and share their story. However, as the years went on that wasn't the case. I get countless people reaching out to me on Instagram every single day, for which an easy 99% of them are women. I can count on one hand the number of men that message me. As mentioned in my story of dealing with masculinity, I am very much aware of the stigma around men showcasing their vulnerabilities. My dad didn't and it killed him. Which I guess is the main reason I am so vocal with my story. Not only to give everyone permission to share their story but to make it very apparent that men need to be vocal also.

A friend of mine, Vlad Negrau, reached out to me and bravely asked if he could share his story inside this book. What I find interesting is that I never knew his story. I never knew he was a survivor of sexual abuse. Some time ago he reached out to me and asked if I had seen a therapist to help me through my trauma, but he never mentioned going through it himself. Which further made me realise that we truly have no idea who is a survivor and who isn't. Who is living in silence and who is not.

So here is Vlad's story below.

"When I was little my parents were always busy, so my way of spending time all day was playing outside, mostly unattended. The emotional negligence of my parents played a major part in laying 'the groundwork' for my abuse. It also led to me developing alexithymia over the years (also known as emotional blindness). The neighbours I played with were between 4 and 7 years older than me. The abuse started when I was 6, by a guy that was 12 years old at that time, I'll name him M. I was exposed to porn, and I was slowly made to believe that all things sexual were perfectly normal, even at my age. That was the introduction. What followed was 2 years of constant exposure to not only porn but also him touching his genitals. When I was about 8 the abuse took another level. A friend of his, I'll name him T (a lot older than me as well), made me give him oral sex. Then M started to ask me for the same thing, even trying to pay me for it. This went on for another 2-3 years... I was groomed into thinking what I was doing was fine, that it was something friends do... a way to show that you care and that you're a good guy. When I was around 11, M took things to another level. He started raping me, and once again acted like it was something normal. I truly believed there's nothing wrong with it until I was about 13. This abuse continued up until I was 15. That's when it stopped because M. moved to another city. He never talked about it, I never talked about it, and even though I knew something was wrong in the last 2 years, I still considered him my best friend - I know, it sounds impossible, but because he groomed me since I was 6, my notion of good and bad was flawed. In fact, I considered him my best friend until recently. I'm 22 now and only 6 months ago I accepted what happened to me and I ended everything with M. Now I'm dealing with a lot of emotions and I have a hard time coping with everything

I've gone through. I spent 90% of the time with him, I spent more time with him than with my parents than at school... because of that, I didn't create long-term relationships or deep relationships with anyone else. I guess that was part of his plan... in his sick mind, he tried to make me his, to keep me only for himself... he tried to make me gay even if that wasn't who I was. I had problems with this, later on, I was wondering if I'm gay because of what happened... but I came to understand that I'm not gay because of what he did to me... I like women and I never even thought about men in that way. The damage M. has done to me is huge and I'm slowly working on building myself up. I have a hard time connecting with people, I can't share my emotions, I'm sceptical of others, I have extreme hatred and anger inside, I'm depressed, I don't see sex as something emotional, and most of all... I'm frustrated about how life started for me. Even so, speaking about the trauma, acknowledging it, and putting it down on paper is helping a lot. Going to therapy, reading books, and materials about what happens in my brain, about other sexual abuse survivors' stories - all these help with my healing. It's a long and harsh road ahead, but each day I'm taking a step forward. Each day I'm trying to connect with my own emotions and accept them. Not running away is the first step any survivor should take. I've run away from this trauma for years and years... but it only made it worse. No matter how bad it hurts, accepting the fact that it happened is necessary for healing. And also finding someone who you can speak with, someone who's there by your side no matter what. I don't know when I would've accepted what happened if it weren't for my girlfriend. She's the one who helped me tap into my emotions and get them out. She accepted me for who I am, she acknowledges my pain and my frustration, and she is always there for me. This person doesn't have to be your partner as in my case, it can be a therapist, a friend, a parent, or anyone else. But no matter what, traumas shouldn't be kept inside, under a lock. If you're in the same boat as I am, or if you've been through a similar experience or any kind of trauma, let your voice be heard. You're not alone."

What's interesting about Vlad's story is the questioning of his own sexual identity. Because his first sexual experiences were with a boy, did that mean he was gay? Did that mean he should be gay? I know this something on the minds of a lot of people, both men and women. So I want to just take a second and tell you that it does not. Whilst there is absolutely no shame in being attracted to the same sex, I don't want you to feel trapped in thinking you need to based on what you have been exposed to. What has happened to you does not form your identity today. You are in the driver's seat. You are in control. You have the power of choice. Whether that means you are straight, gay or bisexual. You are choosing your lane based on what your heart tells you today, not on what the demons in your story are trying to tell you.

Mac Kenzie

"Growing up I tried desperately to hold onto my innocence for as long as I could. I spent a lot of time alone as a child. My home life wasn't the best and I didn't have many if any, friends. I knew that my purpose was not to live my life for the satisfaction of others. I knew that I needed to focus on myself and not worry about what anyone thought of me. Sometimes this logic was hard when I felt like I didn't fit in. However, at the end of the day, the only opinion of me I cared about was Gods.

Growing up mostly in solitude, I came to have a really strong faith. Even though my faith was strong I still was fighting for control of my life. I was making the decisions and overly planning my days. I hadn't given God the reins to my life or stopped trying to make everything go my way, instead of God's way. I wasn't fully relying on God to lead me. Since I am strong in my faith I always planned on saving myself for marriage. I soon realized that I didn't always have control over what happens in my life.

The first time I got sexually abused I was 17 and I was asleep at my grandmother's house. I was in a safe environment that was basically a second home to me. In my sleep, I was molested by a relative and woke up to the act happening. I was not sexually active at the time, so this was very shocking to me. I immediately told my grandma because I knew that abusers will try to make victims seem like they made the scenario up. I laid awake until my brain shut down that night, jolting with fear every time I closed my eyes. I had no idea how to handle this situation emotionally. So, I pushed down my feelings and continued with my life. This incident continues to affect me today. I cannot sleep without a room that has a locked door.

During my first semester of college, my life took a sharp turn. I got invited to a frat party and ended up drinking way too much. I trusted a person I shouldn't have trusted and I ended up getting raped. This was how I lost my virginity. I was so torn up after this incident. Emotions from prior sexual abuse came forward and piled onto the pain I was currently feeling. For about four or five months I became depressed. I cut off all my hair, went from blonde to brunette, and distanced myself from everyone. I would eat half a protein bar a day and constantly push myself to be numb. I just wanted to feel loved and every time I suffered from sexual abuse it felt more and more impossible that could ever happen for me. A few months after I started to get better, I got into a relationship. This relationship soon became mentally, verbally, and physically abusive. The abusive relationship did not help with my previous trauma from the sexual assaults at all. For 11 months I planned on killing myself. I cried every morning I woke up because I knew I needed to fight through another day. I was starving myself and constantly crying. I relied on weed to numb my pain and help me cope with each day. I fell into deep darkness I had never felt before. I felt even more destroyed, dirty, worthless, weak, etc. During my breakup, I made a new friend. He helped me leave my abusive ex-boyfriend for good. However, I didn't realize he had other motives. I had been awake for more than 24 hours, flew on a plane, and I was at the club drinking and smoking until 3 am. Once we got back to the house a group of us were staying at, I was ready to pass out. However, my friend had other plans. I was gripping onto my consciousness and everything I saw was blurry. I couldn't respond to my body because I was so weak. While going through a horrible breakup, I was raped again. After this incident, I was done. I was ready to give up. This sexual assault really stole from me any hope I had left in my heart. For months I was traumatized. I didn't want to go near anyone let alone be touched by anyone.

In November 2019 I was at a point in my life where I was deciding whether to kill myself or stay alive. I knew the only way I would want to stay alive was if God was at the centre of my life. I prayed and talked to God about how I was so ready to die and I needed a sign from him to know that my voice was being heard. That same night God showed himself to me and sent me a sign. I threw my hands up and surrendered my heart to God. I gave over the reins and extended my love and trust into Him. I knew that I was the happiest I had ever been in my life when God was at the centre of it. From that night on I continued to fight for myself. I let myself release all the emotions I needed to. Life wasn't perfect all at once. It took a lot of time and effort to grow and heal myself. I discovered more about myself then I had in so long. I found new hobbies that made me happy. I found a new home church I really love and joined the young adult's group. I have met so many new people and created so many beautiful memories. I spent the last eight months waking up and pouring all my effort into myself and my relationship with God. I sparked that intimacy between God and me in our relationship. I haven't felt this blessed in my entire life. I work out and eat healthy because my body loves it! I do everything I can to make myself happy every day and do what I need to to create a beautiful life for myself.

Today, I wake up and I smile with excitement for the day that lays ahead. My life has been radically changed and I owe it all to the grace and love of Jesus. I am oftentimes very hard on myself. I try and bounce back so fast that I forget how much time it takes to heal my brain from every trauma, not just my body. It is easy for me to forget how far I have come. I suffer every day from the effects of my sexual assaults, but I no longer run from my pain. I am still healing and will continue to heal for the rest of my life, but I didn't give up. I wanted to give up so bad. I felt defeated, weak, and desperate for a breath of fresh air. I didn't want to lie on my death bed anymore. I wanted to make the most out of my days. I wanted to laugh, smile, love, etc. I knew that I couldn't give up because I still had so many things planned for myself. I wanted to get married and have children. I wanted to create a beautiful life for myself, so I didn't give up. Healing is not linear. There will be great days and there will be bad days. What you need to know is that you're not alone and you're strong enough to get through this".

Jacob Kauffman

"In middle school, I was sexually abused at summer camp while I was sleeping by an older high schooler. I woke up to my friends laughing and joking about what had just happened. I can't imagine feeling more alone while being surrounded by so many friends. All I remember thinking was: Why would someone do that? How could the friends I had grown up with my entire life, just sit by and do nothing to stop it? How could they play it off as a joke? It was never a joke to me. I was made fun of for being gay because I'm domesticated AF and am super in touch with my feminine side! ;) #woke.

From then on I never felt fully accepted by my friends. I believed that I needed to prove myself worthy of other people's friendship. I learned to not trust anyone who loved me, because if they loved me, then that meant that they would hurt me. I thought that if I let people see me for who I actually was, they wouldn't accept me. I made up a story that I wasn't enough. So I started to wear masks and I would become all things to all people (even if it meant lying) just to fit in and be liked. It took me 10 years just to acknowledge the event as sexual abuse. And you know what? I'm grateful for it. Being abused was one of the best things that ever could have happened to me. It made me into the man I am today. It made me strong, courageous, fearless, bold, powerful, outspoken, resourceful, independent, creative, expressive, loving, accepting and kind. Being abused allowed me to share my story so others could be inspired and heal from their traumatic experiences. I've been selfish by not sharing my story. Meanwhile, there are over 4,600 young people between the ages of 10-24 that commit suicide every year. Oftentimes for much less than what happened to me.

I'm here to tell you that you are not defined by what happened to you and that you are not alone. You are capable of turning your pain into your purpose to serve others. We need you to break your silence and share your story, lives depend on it."

Jeweliet Tangen

"I was born in Idaho in the late 90s. Very few people know the truth about my life, and most are not ready to hear the details, since it is hard to believe the things I have seen. When I was only 2 months old, my biological mom abandoned me on a doorstep of a foster care house in west Idaho. This horrible place would be my "home" off-and-on for the first 6 years of my life. What I was about to experience is something unexplainable. Most people can't process the reality of what happened at this place in Idaho, even though it's all true.

Just like me, many kids experienced and are still experiencing the same horror I got to go through. Sadly this is a global problem that needs to be addressed. Looking back now, I still can't believe how I managed to get out of that place alive. Some of the kids in the house seemed to be the "favourite", and some were quite obviously the "least favourite". Yet, we all went through horrific experiences. Ones that were favoured would get to go last, which was a welcome spot in line since our tormentors would eventually tire out and get what they wanted from the kids first in line. I wish I could accurately describe the feeling of what it's like to be tortured, but all I can say is that the psychical pain ends. The emotional pain, however, follows you for long after the torture ends.

We felt absolutely hopeless at the mercy of our "caregivers", realising we could never do anything to stop them. We feared death, yet we grew fonder of the idea as we got older as a "welcome relief." On some level, I think I wanted to die and stop the suffering. Today I feel guilty for something that someone else did to us, knowing that it was 100% luck that got me adopted while the rest of the kids had to stay and suffer. What is a kid supposed to believe about the world they live in if everything they have seen is torture, sexual abuse and death? The level of shame and guilt that sexually abused kids experience changes their lives forever. Most people that experience this level of abuse die with this secret, which slowly kills them from the inside.

What I got to see and experience through those days wired my brain in a very particular way. Not many people really understand the way I process information and emotions today. I think I must've built a strong resilience bone during those years, which is how I've been able to be so successful in life now. I don't say that to brag, though. I say that because now, in my early twenties, I've found my "life purpose" if you will and there is no way I'd be able to fulfil this purpose if I hadn't gone through what I have. I saw kids being raped next to me, friends cut open while being tied to a kitchen table, I suffered sexual abuse and torture. I saw grown men and women exploiting a system to fulfil some dark desire for blood and sex with children. But as I said, I got lucky. When I was 6 I was adopted by my mom, Cheryl. She found out about my existence years after she adopted my biological sister, and wanted us to be together. So she took me in, even though she was almost 50, single, and had severe health issues. I remember the day I finally left that horrible place, and honestly, I was equally afraid of leaving with this stranger as I was afraid of staying and continuing to be abused.

I later learned this is called "Stockholm Syndrome." When I got in the car with my mum I was certain that I was being taken away to be killed or that something much more horrific would happen to me. I seriously thought something worse was yet to come. Even after leaving foster care and being with my new family, I felt fear on behalf of my friends that I left behind. My mom and I would pray for the other kids in the foster care house every day. I cried every night for years, hoping that my friends had found some peace. For the first time, I could feel what it was like having a real family. And while that was a wonderful experience, the idea of feeling love or happiness was foreign. I resisted and developed a significant fear of anything "good."

After a while, I got comfortable with my new family and I can say that this was the best I had ever felt. I felt loved for the first time in my life! My mom and I spent almost all our time together. She taught me what love was, and how to forgive. She taught me how to make the best out of any situation. I spent a lot of time taking care of her as she was very sick and depressed most of my childhood, but I was incredibly happy to do so. To me, this woman not only saved my life, but she taught me about something I never thought I'd feel... Love and happiness. My mom passed away 8 years after she adopted me, just six days before my 15th birthday. And of all the things I've endured, losing my mom was by far the hardest experience of my life. After my mum died, my family broke apart and I spent the next 2 years moving from one house to another. While grateful some people had offered to help me after my mom passed, I realized quickly that if nothing in my life changed, I would end up like an average kid who had been through trauma. I knew I wanted more. So I managed to get myself a job as a waitress while attending college at the same time. That didn't last long. Probably because I hate being told what to do, and I resented the idea of ending up average. So, by 16 I started my first business as a freelance copywriter and landed an important client in France, whom I still serve today. In business, I found a way to escape the world. It was easier. There was black and white, cause and effect relationships. It also required resilience and discipline, a skill which I had in spades since I was a child. It's also my resilience that led me to be so successful, so quick. While everyone was stuck on small details, disappointed with every rejection, and lacking discipline, I thrived.

By the age of 20, I had already become a millionaire. Business became my passion, and I learned a very important lesson early on... The more I made the more people and kids I could help. This is what keeps me motivated. After 6 years in business, doing a variety of things, I was awarded the Business Woman of the year 2019 in San Diego. One of my companies, The Strategy Loft, has become one of the fastest-growing companies in its space and I have already donated over one million dollars to charities, helping kids all over the world. I had to learn the hard way that it doesn't matter how bad things get, they can always get worse. I learnt that there's always something to be grateful for. I believe there's a reason for everything, and if I made it through this hell, while many others didn't, it must be because I need to do something about it. The images of these kids being tortured and slaughtered, the images of all this blood and pain, haunt me every day. I know most people struggle to believe this, and I don't blame them. If I hadn't experienced all this myself, I would also be hesitant to believe that something this horrific is still happening today, all over the world. I believe that all the pain and horror I witnessed has given me a unique perspective and skill set to be able to help adults and children who are still being affected by these horrible acts. It's also coincidentally, probably why I've been so successful even at such a young age. Most don't live through an experience as I have, and now my mission is to prevent it from happening to as many future kids as possible. I've thought a lot about the future and what I want. I love the life I have now and I enjoy my own success. But my motto for years has been, "make more, so you can give more." And now it's my time to give back.

UNNAMED 1

"Hello to anybody that is reading this. I am breaking my silence on the abuse I went through as a child not necessarily for me, but for the person who needs to know that they aren't alone and they have the strength inside of them to get through this, even if they feel like they don't. I have struggled with writing this because it is hard to write about. I was also debating not putting it out here, but I did, and I hope it helps.

So here is my story...

My biological mother neglected me from the day I was born. But even before that, she drank during her pregnancy with me, and that has impacted my growth. There is a syndrome called foetal alcohol syndrome, which is caused by a mother drinking heavily while she is pregnant. I have some of the symptoms like learning difficulties and physical differences, but you would not notice them unless you were looking for it. I have been diagnosed with dyslexia and hyper motor ability, or more commonly known as dyspraxia. My mother would leave me in the house for hours alone with my brother when I was only a baby, and when he was a child. My mum would send me to school with clothes that would not fit me and nits in my hair, so I was always itchy, and I wouldn't be fed properly so I was underweight too. My mum even refused to get help for me regarding my education and my learning difficulties. She manipulated me, and she did not care for me or protect me at all. She failed me as a mum. She had an affair which led to my parents splitting up and getting a divorce. That one choice had a massive impact on me, my brother and then eventually, the rest of my family. My mum moved in with her new partner and my brother, and I lived with them. My mum's partner had two sons, one slightly older than me, and the other one was the same age as my biological brother. I never felt safe being at mums, but that was my normal, and when things are terrible, you go into survival mode, which is what I did. So, there are things I do not remember because it was so traumatic, I just blocked a lot of it out. I remember not being good enough. I was always doing something wrong and everything would be my fault. I remember not feeling safe and walking on eggshells all the time. I remember my mum's partner's sons would physically abuse me. My mum said it was my fault because I was winding them up. I have some scars that were caused by them.

I remember being emotionally abused by my mums' partner as well. He abused me because of my issues with school and my struggles with reading. He told me always I was stupid and not smart enough. He forced me to read to him and I hated every moment of that because I had to be close to him. He would force me to eat super spicy chillies and I would sit there and cry. My mum just let it happen. He would work day and night shifts, so most of the time it would only be me and him in the house on the weekends until late afternoon. It would be horrible when he would work night shifts because he would always blame me for waking him up. He would say that I was being too noisy every time, without fail. He would also call my dad names and my dad's partner horrible names all time. He would cause arguments and would scream and shout for no apparent reason. Whilst at my mums, my eldest brother was my safe place. I trusted him. He picked me up from school every day, he looked after me and tried to protect me as much as he could. However, he went on to sexually abuse me on three separate occasions. The first time was on holiday with my grandparents (who were my mums' parents). We got told off for using too much water. My brother put the shower on to make our grandparents think that someone was using it. The second time was at my dad's house. I was getting ready for bed and he came into my room and made me do stuff to him. The other time was on holiday with my grandparents in a caravan. That was the worst out of the three occasions because I remember how it happened and what he said to me. We were sharing a room, even though there was a spare one, but my big gran said I had to be in the other room with him because there was an age difference (which I don't understand now that I think about it). I remember him speaking to me about it like we were just having a normal conversation. I remember after it happened I went into the toilet because I felt sick. Afterwards, I would have to return to the same room so I could sleep. He told me to keep it quiet, and I kept quiet because I trusted him. I thought he would never do anything to hurt me because he was my older brother. I didn't know it was wrong. However, I believe deep down in my core that I knew it was wrong. But I kept my silence on it until one day at school, in year 4 or 5, I was told we would be learning about sex education. They mentioned a few things that made me confused. I was like "what? Why are we talking about this? I have done this already?" in my head. I was so confused. I turned to my friends and I told them about what happened to me, and I begged them to keep it quiet because in my head I broke a promise to my brother. The next day my whole world changed and was flipped upside down. I came to school like any typical day, but my teacher had a meeting with my headteacher, and I knew in my stomach it was about me. I was so nervous and scared about what was going to happen. I did not know what to do. My teacher came back from the meeting and asked me to go with her. She told me I was not in trouble, they just wanted to speak to me. My mum was brought into the school to see me and child services were there, and they spoke to me and asked me questions about what happened. I remember them telling me that my brother was going to stay somewhere else. At that moment, and I did for a long time, I felt so guilty because I felt like my family was being torn apart because of what I said. However, I knew something was not right because this would not be happening if it was okay or normal. The courts and child services dealt with it all. I still don't know much about that process at all because my stepmom and dad protected me from it. So yes, in the eyes of law, justice was found in my case. However it didn't deal with all of my emotional trauma, and I didn't get closure from that aspect of it in the long run just because I was so young.

My journey of healing from all of that was long, and I am still not fully there yet. However, my stepmom was the best thing that happened to me. She helped me so much through it all. She helped me with my education, my confidence, my emotions, my hurt and my self-harm. She fought for me to have a better life. She fixed me and listened to my cries and my endless conversations about everything that had gone on, and still does. She read me books and reassured me it was not my fault, and showed me a normal childhood. She fought for me to have a counsellor to help me process everything and know that it was not my fault. She was the mum I always needed, and I call her my mum now. I have dealt with a lot of my emotional scars and have gained some closure within the last year or so. I didn't care for what my stepbrothers did to me because that didn't bother me. I knew it was wrong, but they were just not nice people. Plus, what they did was nothing compared to the most significant issues I had to deal with. So, I was able to square it away pretty easy.

My issues with my mum were the most difficult one to move on from because she questioned my worth so much, and I had to accept an apology I would never get. She was in my life for a while because I wanted some type of relationship with her. However, when my dad won parental rights for me, I lived with them. I was removed from her toxic behaviours and was shown a healthy functioning, loving, supportive family. I saw my mum at the weekend. She would make me lie about things that happened then, and I would have to deal with her partner, but I made that sacrifice to see my mum. We would occasionally have a nice time. We would bake now and then. My brother stayed over one time when I was at my mums, which wasn't allowed because of everything that had happened, and she told me to keep it quiet for a week or so. My self-harming was terrible at the time because I was following another secret and I was yet again conflicted. One time my mum was supposed to pick me up after school but she never turned up. She left me in the pouring rain, no text, no phone call or anything. That was the moment I realised I couldn't have her in my life anymore. We went our separate ways until I turned 18 and at this point, I knew what she was still like. But I was holding on to hope that she would have changed, and she would love me and be the mum I always wanted. But also, that she would listen to me. I had questions and things I did not understand. When we got into a conversation and I confronted her about the things that truly hurt me, she told me lies and tried to manipulate me. She completely ignored and blocked me on everything. She rejected me once again.

What my mum's partner did to me took a while to get closure for because I believed for a long time that I was stupid. That I wasn't good enough and that I wouldn't make it. Over time whilst I was living with my dad and my stepmom, they taught me I could do anything I put my mind to. So, I used what he said to me to motivate me and to push myself to prove him wrong, and I did. I did still doubt myself from time to time, but for someone who was not smart enough or good enough on an academic level, I did surprisingly good. I could not read or write in year six; however, I got eleven GCSEs with 2 A's and the rest B's and C's. I started to believe in myself and what I could do. I was off to sixth form to study my chosen subjects and I set my targets high, not for them but for myself to prove that I could do it. I also proved to myself that I could succeed in sports. I built on my confidence as I got chosen to represent my county at 18 for contact rugby. This had been my target for that year to play county, and I did it. I was pleased and proud of myself for it. When I realised I was not controlled by him any longer was when he tried to manipulate me to speak to my mum. He told me I should be an adult in the situation as I turned 18 years old. I cut ties with my mum for a long time and still have. I told him that was not going to happen and I stood my ground. I told him I don't care about him and confronted him about what he did to me. I was not going to be that scared little child I was back then, and I was not going to let him manipulate me yet again. That was when I knew I wasn't afraid of him anymore.

As for my brother, well, weirdly when I look back this was easier to move on from. I was confused by what he did at first, then I felt guilty and that it was my fault. Then I was angry that it happened to me. What was it about me that deserved all this hurt and pain? I self-harmed for ages by picking my skin until it bled. It was all over my body, but mainly my legs because it was easier to hide. I used to wear jeans all the time, and jumpers, or just anything to cover me up. I wouldn't show off my legs or just wear vest tops. I hated doing it because I felt vulnerable. My stepmom started pushing me to wear more girlie clothes out in public to get me more comfortable within my skin. I began to question why my brother did what he did the older I got. I had conversations with him about it. I understand that his life was hard, and mum neglected him. He was emotionally abused by mum's partner, which is part of the reason why he did what he did to me, to prove himself to his abuser. My brother tried to get in touch with and to get back into my life. He was talking to me like normal, but I found it weird and awkward because of what had happened. So, I told him that we needed to have a conversation about everything. I got it all off my chest. I said how he hurt me and the pain he has caused. He listened and accepted it. He apologised for it all and shortly afterwards, I decided that I could forgive him for what he did. We both agreed to try and work on building our brother and sister relationship.

So yes, I was a victim of sexual abuse, neglect, physical and emotional abuse, but I am not a victim. I am a survivor, and I am so proud of the person I am today, and all the adversity have faced. I know I am good enough, I am strong enough, I am smart enough, and I know you are too! I still struggle from time to time with believing it, but I look at how far I have come. I promise these bad times will get better but do not be hard on yourself for feeling the way you do because this is not an easy journey, and it is fine to feel that way. Your story may be different or like mine, but that is your story, and you will get through this no matter what your journey looks like."

UNNAMED 2

"A night with my best friend since kindergarten turned into one of the worst days of my life. It all started when one of the cutest boys from my high school sent me a text me, a chubby and unpopular girl. Obviously, my anxiety went through the roof when he asked me if I wanted to hang out with him and I told my best friend how afraid I was and she told me to take some of her "anxiety medication." The last thing I truly remember was her helping me into his truck and it all went blurry until the last thing I saw was the moon. Now my innocence was already taken before that when my mother would let her boyfriends take advantage of me and the abuse I suffered from her.

The abuse from my mother started with smacking and led to her lighting my hair on fire, cutting me, and cutting me off from the outside world, all very cruel things to do to a little girl. This caused me to have severe depression, PTSD, and histrionic personality disorder. This caused me to drop out of high school, push away from family and friends, and self-harm.

Life was not easy after sexual abuse but it's not impossible. I found a lot of great resources at a mental facility I went to, watching Perry/other trauma survivors, and going back to college for something

I love to do! My family wasn't always supportive, a lot of them didn't even believe my trauma because I hid it behind a smile. But I found courage after seeing that sadly, but honestly, I'm not the only person this kind of stuff happens too and I shouldn't end my life over something I couldn't control and so many people have to suffer through! I decided to go into counselling to use and channel my past/personal experiences to help others going through the same thing. I hope everyone knows you're not alone and can find new ways to cope with your trauma."

UNNAMED 3

"Where do I start? When you have something traumatic trapped in a box inside your head and keeping it in there for 13 years dealing with it on a day to day basis even though I am 29 with a child...

Okay, here it goes.

I never had my father in my life, so I looked up to a man that my mum was seeing as my stepfather. He married her. My 1st abuse was when I was 9. I remember lying down on my belly on the floor watching tv with a nightie on, and I remember seeing him there on the sofa. Then I was talking to him about something (can't remember what) and I was focusing on the tv. Then I felt something go up my leg. I was scared. I looked down and it was his hand. I didn't know what was happening and he rubbed. My mum came down from upstairs, I ran out and upstairs to my room, confused about what just happened. I used to play outside a lot when he was there. I stayed over at my mate's house as much as I could. It stopped for a while when I was in Comprehensive school, and then it started again. A cuddle before school always turned into touching me, playing with me, and if my mum was working late he would use toys. And the sad part about it... I stayed over at my mate's house one day for school and I looked and thought to myself, "why isn't her dad doing the same things to her that I was getting?".

I didn't understand it, but it felt like a routine in the end. I ended up hanging myself but I did it wrong and the dog lead came undone. Then things started getting weird. Like, he would come into my room and look at me. I got scared and had enough of him coming into my room. I had dreams that I would lash out and would punch him in the face because he was that close to me. I played on the Xbox a lot if I wasn't out. My mum would shout at me and he would put a wedge in between us. So if I were to say "Mum?", she would shout "WHAT?!" in a moody voice. But when I was 16 I had enough. But by this time I was thinking and telling my closer mates, "Is this normal?" and they would tell me that I needed to tell my mum. But I couldn't because I was scared that he would kill her, which he would use as a threat for everything. It was always walking on eggshells with him. But I eventually told my mum's best friend, and I went to Ireland where my Nan was living. At the time I was terrified. I would ring my mum all the time to check-in with her. Funny enough I would even text her when she was going out just to see where she was because I still get scared to this day. It never went to court and the man is still driving around to this day.

I was having nightmares and screaming out in my sleep for months after. I started self-harming for which the doctor then transferred me to see a counsellor. So after I told someone about it, it was weird because by that time I was in college trying to carry on with my life. Be "normal" I guess. People who know about it would act like "Awww, love her" or "That's the girl that got abused". My abuser would turn up at college and beep his horn, tormenting me. I had to take a few weeks off college. I didn't tell him when I went back to college and did another 2 years there. So the day came for me to see a counsellor. I was scared but it was the best thing I did. I got the "Why me?!" answers and everything else.

I still got a book that I need to burn to let that part of my life go. But it never goes. Just, we all have different coping skills and I found if you write everything down, even write to the younger you now, what would you say? I would write "I am proud of you for being a beautiful woman and mum you have become. I know the flashbacks come back every now and then, and your mental health can be a tool, but never knock yourself. You do it gal. Keep that chin up".

UNNAMED 4

"So around 10 years ago I was in a reasonably long term relationship. He was my first love. My first time when I was just 14. I loved him with all my heart. I trusted him with my entire world. But He took control of my life. I couldn't talk to anyone unless he approved them. He checked my phone. He made me delete my friends so I had no one around me except him. Obviously, we were having sex regularly. Only, one evening about 2 years into the relationship he wanted it. I said no, over and over. It still happened. I froze. I couldn't do anything. I guess at first I didn't even realise what was happening. I didn't realise it was actually rape. I didn't want it to happen and he knew that. He told me it was ok and normal. I knew deep down it wasn't. I cry regularly. I drink to blur my feelings. I remember everything and it hurts. He raped me. But I still stayed with him for a further year! That has fucked my life so much. It has screwed any form of relationship with anyone. I don't trust anyone. I have suppressed my feelings for so long. I have been killing myself for 10 years. I have self-harmed. I have drunk myself stupid. I have said my goodbyes to my mum and told her I loved her and parked my car in front of canals with the intent of driving into it. It kills me every. Single. Day. It's ruining my current relationship even though I try to stop it. And it's ruining any chance of friendships I could potentially

have.

I'm reluctant to meet anyone. While I want to trust people, I trusted him with my whole world and he ruined my life. To this day I blame myself for not fighting. And I'm so scared to get into that situation again. But the worst thing is, I still stayed with him. I still let him control me. Even after we split up he still controlled me. Then I became friends with him and his new partner so he could control me even more. And it wasn't until last year when everything finally became too much. When I started drinking more, killing myself to feel something. It took a lot to bring myself back. But all I ever wanted was to tell the world and not be judged. But I can't. I can't tell my family because they would literally kill him for what he did."

UNNAMED 5

"I have no idea how I'm supposed to put some of the worst years of my life in a few paragraphs, but I'll start from who he was. I met him when I was 6 when I became friends with his younger sister and we all became great friends, spending all our time together. But once I started sleeping over, he began taking advantage of me. As she would fall asleep he would take me to his room and ask if I wanted to play a game. It would begin by daring me to do something stupid to kissing him, and from there it simply progressed. In the end, he made me take off all my clothes whilst he touched me and made me touch him. I'd close my eyes and cry hoping it would all be over soon. This went on for 6 years. But as I got older I began trying to fight back, but that felt pointless because it then just became more violent.

I always felt guilty, ashamed and dirty after it happened but one of the worst feelings as being powerless. So one night I told myself I wasn't going to let it happen. So when he began by putting his hand on my leg I pushed him away but then he got annoyed and climbed on top of me pinning me down, putting his hand up my skirt and trying to take off my underwear. He took his pants off then his sister woke up and sent him out of the room and the rest of the night was a blur. I just remember waking up with bruises up and down my legs and arms and blood in my underwear. I'm still unsure what happened for the rest of the night but part of me wonders if something else might have happened and I blocked it out.

After that incident I stopped going around, I'm not sure why I hadn't before then. Since then I've battled with depression and anxiety trying to keep it a secret. Each day just merged into one constantly faking a smile or a laugh. But as soon as I was home I would go straight to the kitchen and pick up a pair of scissors or a knife to self-harm with. Because the pain of cutting hurts less than everything else. I couldn't sleep because of nightmares and I was having panic attacks nearly every day. Numerous times it got so unbearable I tried to commit suicide. But each time I thought of my family and convinced myself it would get better. And I was right, it does get better. I finally broke my silence and told my friend and then eventually my parents. They all helped me the best they could and got me therapy for the parts they couldn't help with. My Councilor taught me how to identify things and not suppress them. So each time a panic attack happens, it helps to write it down so I can look back on it later. And by doing this I can learn how to prevent them. Then with each day it slowly gets better, some days there are setbacks but when I look at the bigger picture my life is so much better. I have a boyfriend who I love, and I'm doing well in school. My life is finally getting back on track but with the added benefit that I'm stronger and it's shaped me into the person I am today. And for that, I'm proud of myself".

UNNAMED 6

"From a young age, I was sexually abused. I ended up living with a different and loving family at 10 years old. Then effects the abuse had on me started to hit in my teen years. I spoke to who I now call my parents, who have helped me through all my difficult times. I reported my sexual abuse to the police, but there was a lack of evidence. I felt as if everything that happened was my fault. I used to hurt myself just to numb the pain I was in. I stopped hurting myself with the help of my family. It took me years to get stronger. My mum thinks I'm doing a lot better from what I went through. I will never be able to change what happened to me, but I can change my future."

UNNAMED 7

"I used to think surviving rape was all about tears, shame and keeping quiet. So when it happened to me 20 years ago, this is exactly what I did. It was a normal summer day. It was what it started out to be, the school was over, the sun was shining and I was excited for another day of running, screaming and playing. Little did 7 year old me know that this was going to be the summer from hell. My assault happened in 2001 when both my parents had gone to Pakistan for my grandfather's funeral and me and my younger sister were left with our aunt. It was a busy house with 7 cousins ranging from 19 to 6. I woke up as normal like I did every morning and went downstairs to breakfast and then came back upstairs to brush my teeth. My older cousin dressed me and helped me brush my teeth and sent me on my way to go play with the others. The day went on and I found myself sitting in front of the television on my own watching CBBC (for those that don't know what this is, it is a children's television channel here in the UK owned by the BBC). At this moment my cousin who was at the time 18 years old came into the room and asked me if I wanted to play a game. I innocently nodded my head and followed him upstairs. The house was quiet, I could hear children outside laughing and the ice cream truck pulls up. I asked him "can I get ice cream Bhai (brother)?", to which he

replied, "if you win this game then I'll get you loads of ice cream".

I scuttled into the room as he shut the door behind me and picked me up onto the bed, I thought nothing of it. That's when my jeans were lowered, I was pushed into the mattress and a sock was put into my mouth, I started to panic and cry as he forced himself on me. Seconds felt like hours, he walked me to the bathroom as he cleaned me and told me "if you tell anyone then I'm going to do it again". I ran downstairs and out into the garden, it happened again the next day, and the day after and the day after. It wasn't till my parents came back that it was over. I thought I had done something wrong, that this had happened when you were punished. I went on to find myself at the age of 11 with 2 friends on a trail behind my grandmother's house where they both sandwiched themselves against me pulling my hair and forcing me onto my knees and up against the fence and the wall.

2 friends turned to 1, he would come to my house every day and ask if I could come out and had I refused it was a punch in the stomach or a slap in the face when he would later get a hold of me. It became normal to allow him to hurt me and use me, in the shower, in bed, in the garden, in the park, in the bushes, wherever he took me I obliged. It was at this point where I began to explore my sexuality, I came across Grindr and started speaking to guys, on the odd occasion I met them and they would do their business and leave. It left me feeling dirty and disgusted.

I would walk home crying and begging God for forgiveness and promised him it would not happen again. I thought I would get pregnant. I saw my life as an outsider, I laughed, I played, I joked but it brought me no satisfaction. I felt alone and alienated. I found myself cutting myself, it relieved the pain watching the blood trail down my arm, it felt like the pain was leaving my body as it dripped off my arm. It made me feel in control for a moment. A time where I controlled what happened and I didn't have to listen to anyone else. Years went on as I found myself cutting my arms and my legs until I met an amazing guy in college at age 19. We talked and bonded and he shared with me that he too was raped, this is when I knew I was not alone. That there are others out there like me.

Coming from a Pakistani Kashmiri Muslim background, you can't be gay, you don't talk about rape. It's taboo. If that happens, you keep quiet. You butch up because boys must be boys and girls must be girls. And to this day I have never openly admitted that I was raped to any of my family for the fear of being cast out. However, I feel I am no longer scared of what the future holds for me. It's a long road ahead but I walk it with my head held high."

UNNAMED 8

"No one can make you feel inferior without your consent." – Eleanor Roosevelt. Words I'd soon come to realise, although profound in its own right, have merit.

What can I say, a safe healthy childhood is what every child should have. It should be a right, but alas, some of us are not so lucky. We are born, experiencing things that should never be, and the overall repercussions either make or break the spirit. My story is somewhat along the usual path. The predator meets the child under conventional circumstances and takes advantage of the child's innocence, leaving the child to have severe social issues and anxiety. It all started at the age of 11, my family and I had moved to a rather shady neighbourhood due to our extenuating circumstances. This was basically, where we lived for 7 years, where I succumbed to a rude awakening that no child should bear.

I was on the brink of being a teen growing up planning what I aspire to be with the intent of breaking whatever barriers that may come. But what transpired was way beyond anyone's expectations much less mine. These incidents started when I was 11, you see, in the neighbourhood, we were in was more or less out of some movie. Far from the norms, I was accustomed to in my previous home. Neighbours whose kids I rode bikes with enjoying my childhood playing in the street, fishing at a river mouth, wheelies, video games and such was basically the average 90's kid. But in our new neighbourhood, we were confined to our house as the neighbourhood was not as safe as my parents would have liked it to be. With that in my family befriended a few neighbours not really looking like the conventional adults I was accustomed to being around. Well dressed and looked at children as if they were their own. That was what I would have expected of an adult I would have met thereafter; sadly this was not always the case, a lesson no child should learn that will compromise their innocence.

This individual used to be invited nearly every time my family had a get-together, and sometimes just visit. The assumption was, he's just the next-door neighbour, in being a good neighbour, we tried to be hospitable, and little did I know that I was inviting that darkness into my life. He was never married, nor had kids, just lived at home with his siblings. He did not seem that suspicious, at least to me anyway, then again how was I to know? So, I seem to figure it was whenever I was alone in any part of the house he would find me. At first, it started as a friendly hug, eventually, his hands would have progressed to other parts of me and he would take my hand and place it on his nether regions, asking me if 'I liked what I'm feeling and that I am to play with it.' This would have gone on for the latter part of 5 ½ years and each encounter more daring than the first. Odd thing is, at the time I never saw what he was doing, saying it's all my fault for everything, apart from being a perv he was skilled at manipulation. I doubted myself at times but after it became a topic in one of my classes, I began to do research and eventually succumbed to the realization I was not at fault, it was he who was the predator.

Immediately, things for me started falling into place, my family said we had to move and with this step, I felt relief, and that I was going to get back some sort of sanity and control in my life. At this point, I began to re-evaluate myself at 17, and thought I'd never see him again. So this gave me confidence and newfound gumption, something that was new territory to me and one night I called him and confronted him. With that phone call, I just began to vent explaining how much I hated him, how dirty he made me feel and, well, a few quips about his parents but nonetheless, I sought to battle that demon and he was very quiet and somewhat surprised. I had intended never to see him again and sought to take this to my funeral pyre because I always believed this is something one doesn't bring up in society and the connotations attached are damning mainly for the victim, or at least so I thought. The effects it had on me growing up were interesting. I was already an introvert and with the advent of this, I became reclusive, withdrawn. I started acting out in ways that made me think there was something insidiously wrong with me, exploring stuff in the occult, trying to find myself in the weirdest of ways. I was of the sound opinion that I was at fault. At 15, I tried to overdose on a huge bottle of Tylenol, I figured life itself would have been better without me. Fortunately, all I got was ill and threw up everything the next morning. I kept trying to hurt myself until one day, I thought to myself - "Why punish myself for something I had no control over?" It took some time for this to sink in but the effect it had overflowed into other areas of my life, unfortunately. I was so depressed and sad all the time that I could not focus on school, I found it hard to concentrate as a result, I was flunking everything except Art and Home Economics where I was able to forget everything and just cook and express myself.

The lasting effect of my experiences has altered my perception of the world, to the extent whereby I find it very difficult to open up to people. As a result, I keep people at a distance and as far as relationships go, they never last as I'm left with this stigma of mistrusting everyone I meet. I suffice, some part of me has this self-destructive mode where I always try to ruin things for myself, because I believe subconsciously I'm undeserving of the happiness that most people fight for, I guess part of me still hasn't forgiven myself because I was so naïve and let a stranger take advantage of me. In time, I grew and reintroduced myself to my faith; started praying and meditating which calmed the storms conjuring within and eventually the shadows of that aspect of my past began to be a lot less traumatic with time. Being a Hindu, I found solace in my traditions and focusing my energies on my prayers, fasting and basically channelling that negative energy towards something better to fuel my ambition. After a couple of years, I started feeling better about myself and began putting myself out there again, just now I have limited tolerance for nonsense. But then again, in today's dating world that's an asset. All said and done I am still a 'Work in Progress' trying to be a better person as I refuse to let my past define my future. I once read a quote by Steve Maraboli – " My past has not defined me, destroyed me, deterred me, or defeated me; it has only strengthened me."

With these words in mind, I seek to find peace one day. Each day is a struggle to be a better person and my convictions fuel my resolve to move on. I still strongly believe that no child should ever experience this period. It is a sickness and I pray that these offenders seek help.

If my humble account can help someone find solace in the fact that they are not alone in this struggle, I will then have accomplished something good if at all."

Your Story

When you're ready, come back to this page and write out your story in the space below. This is your time to break your silence.

III

Part 3. Your Story

Owning Your Story

"Owning your story is the bravest thing you'll ever do" - Brene Brown

After reading through all these stories you could be in a whirlwind of emotions. But whatever you are feeling right now, I want you to acknowledge it. Don't ignore it. Every single one of these people, including me, felt like you are feeling right now. Which is exactly why you should break your silence. But before we get onto that, I want to cover the most important step to get to the point of speaking out, and that's about owning your story.

It's about taking full ownership over what happened to you and allowing yourself to actually spend time in that chapter of your life, rather than brush it under the carpet. When we ignore our trauma, we are allowing ourselves to be extremely vulnerable to the repercussions of it, often acting as 'triggers'. Let me ask you this, can you think back to a time where you randomly lashed out at someone? Do you remember doing something, or having a sudden wave of emotion that seemed to come out of nowhere? Maybe some of the times reminding you of the trauma? That's because a trigger (which you weren't likely aware of) happened that caused you to react in a certain way. Unless resolved, you'll further be living in silence, constantly at war with your own inner demons. And what do you think this does when there is a constant war going on inside your body? It sends your stress levels through the roof. You only have to do a google search to see the implications of living in a world of stress, my dad being the epitome of it. So if we are not owning our story, then we are allowing these triggers to act as chains wrapped around us, pinning us down and sabotaging us at any given moment. But the way for us to own our story is to truly accept and acknowledge what happened to us. Which can often be the hardest challenge, but it's also the most courageous. I knew that I had no other option but to own my story when I realised that I could never outrun it. It was then I realised that what had happened could never be undone, but what could be changed was how I dealt with it.

There is no one single way to own your story, but hopefully, you can take what resonates with you the most from this book and allow it to guide you towards the place of ownership. Remember that everything here is geared towards bringing you to the place of breaking your silence. Speaking out when you haven't owned your story yet is extremely difficult to do, mostly because to even mutter the words out loud there has to be some awareness around knowing what actually happened to you. Which is something that most victims of abuse try to hide away from. Which then over time leads to a disconnection from our own self. We spend all our time living out other people's stories instead of writing our own. We get lost and float through life aimlessly because we don't know who we are. But when we can own our story, that's when we can write a new beginning. That's when we start the journey of healing and can start to be in touch with our state of being, without any outside influence.

What owning our story also allows us to do is become super aware of our thoughts and actions that do not serve us, in the present and also when they arise in the future. When I first owned my story, I thought I had it all sorted out. I thought I was all healed up. I was making huge improvements in every area of life. I was much happier, my level of consciousness was constantly expanding, I felt more alive as the days went on and then it came to a point when I met a girl. I fell head over heels in love with this girl, I would have done absolutely anything for her. Then we broke up and I was in pieces. I was in denial and then I was in search mode, trying to look for answers. And then to top it all off, coronavirus lets loose and self-quarantine happened. It was in the exact moment where I knew I still had wounds open from my past traumas (a level of awareness I would have not had if I chose to never own my story). I was locked in my home 23 hours a day (this was the UK law) and my past demons ambushed me. I became extremely suicidal and had some of my darkest days I've ever experienced. It felt like I was all alone with my two sidekicks, loneliness and rejection. Having my partner leave me surfaced these trapped emotions that I never knew existed, and it became unbearable. I either wanted to crash my car, overdose on drugs or hang myself. I didn't want to be in a world where I was loved or accepted. But because I had owned my story, in a brief moment where I was in control, I realised why I was feeling those emotions. It was because growing up I was always fighting for my dad's love and approval, which he rarely gave to me. Well, he did, but not in the way I could understand (Gary Chapman calls it our 'Love Languages'.) Also with my biological mother leaving when I was 4 years old and only seeing her once or twice a year for several years, that played a part too. So once I found someone with which I thought I'd spend the rest of my life with, and I was certain in that fact, I dropped all my guards and became dependent on her. She would give me love and approval in a way I wanted to receive it and she wasn't going to leave as my mum did, and also my dad. So when that all came crashing down, so did my sense of self. But the awareness I then soon had allowed me to work on those vulnerable areas and fall even deeper into spirituality.

A big part of owning your story is showcasing the parts of yourself that make you unique without any expectations. It's showing your flaws and vulnerabilities that you would otherwise tuck away. It's when you deny your story which then allows your ego to take over, that you only showcase the best parts of you with an expectation in return (be it praise, approval, status or recognition). Inside every one of us is our inner child. It's our younger self sitting inside us. And we can either neglect our inner child or we can build a meaningful relationship with it. Denying our story is denying the very existence of our inner child. If you felt neglected as a child in some way, then those feelings are still trapped inside of you because that is what your inner child is currently experiencing by you not communicating with it. How can you expect deep meaningful relationships with others if you can't have one with the one person in the world, you? Your inner child is an extension of you.

A Buddhist once said, "*inside each of us is a young, suffering child and that to protect ourselves from future suffering, we all try to forget the pain. Most often, when we feel pain from a deep place within, it's our inner wounded child who's calling. Forgetting the pain results in more pain."*

The baggage that we hold onto and carry from our childhood can be extremely difficult to unload, especially when it becomes part of our identity. Which is when the art of letting go comes into play, which we will get onto soon.

So make it an utmost priority for you to form a new relationship with your inner child. Because breaking your silence may just be the voice that it needed to hear.

EXERCISE

Use the spaces below to answer each question as best you can.

Do you currently feel like you are owning your story? Why?

When was the last time you were triggered? How and where do you think it's linked to in your story?

How do you feel knowing that you have an inner child within you? What are you going to do about it moving forward?

Forgiveness

"To forgive is to set a prisoner free and discover that prisoner was you" - Lewis B. Smedes

The next step is forgiveness. If you can take full ownership and find forgiveness, you'll be leaps and bounds ahead of where you were, to begin with. Forgiveness is the holy grail of healing, and the path to it is different for everyone. For some, it could be a conscious decision, and for others, it could be a long and winding road. For me, it was a conscious decision when it came to my dad. But for my grandad, it was a bit of a longer process. Only coming to the final destination of forgiveness once I allowed myself to hear and understand his story. But what I will say is this. I'm not saying you must forgive your abuser. If you can forgive yourself and you find you can move forward, then great. Do that. It's just that for me, I wasn't able to. I forgave myself for not speaking out and letting the abuse happen. But I still couldn't move forward. I still blamed my grandad for abusing me, for abusing my dad, and for abusing at least two other people. Because I blamed him, I was still held back. I was still carrying around negative energy which would have impacted areas of my life without me knowing. So I accepted the idea of finding forgiveness towards my grandad so that I can release the energy that wasn't serving me. Like I said earlier in this book, I never wanted to forgive him for his sake. He was dead anyway, so it wouldn't have made an ounce of difference to him. I wanted to forgive him for me so that I could move forward and not let anger or resentment get in the way of me living a happy and fulfilled life. I didn't want it to get in the way of helping other survivors. Sometimes it takes every fibre of your being to forgive someone, but when you realise you are doing it for the greater good, the feat becomes more bearable.

Understand that the person who abused you had a set of beliefs, they had a worldview that made it okay to abuse you. They were conditioned (whether it be through their abuser, parenting, or through some other means) to believe what they were doing was acceptable. Understand that the world they are living in is completely different from the world that you are living in. This person can rape and abuse people because, in their own mind, they have made it acceptable. They have sold themselves a story which they truly believe. So if you can come in from this level of understanding and awareness, you may find it easier to forgive them or the situation. We struggle to forgive when we think the other person is operating from the same frequency as us, thinking "I wouldn't sexually abuse someone, so why would he?" But remember this, someone who abuses someone else has been abused (in some way) themselves. Whether they would like to admit it or not. They are inflicting a similar pain onto others which they once felt and didn't deal with. So if you can shift your perspective to knowing that everyone makes decisions based on their own level of rationalisation, it makes it a little easier to let go.

During the apartheid in South Africa, Nelson Mandela was imprisoned by the white population. The non-whites were tortured and treated in a way no human being should ever be treated. But once Nelson Mandela came out of imprisonment after 27 years, he faced the reality of leading those whom he had fought against for years. Whilst most would come out seeking revenge, Nelson instead chose to forgive the apartheid regime and spoke out saying, *"The time for the healing of the wounds has come. The moment to bridge the chasms that divide us has come. The time to build is upon us."* Mandela was awarded the Nobel Peace Prize in 1993 for exemplifying forgiveness. It would have been a whole lot easier if Mandela did not forgive. But he knew that living through forgiveness is how you beat the demons that are otherwise trying to attack you.

I do want to touch on the possible downside of forgiveness, and that's other people. Whilst many of the black population arguably did not agree with Mandela's notion of forgiveness, you may have the same when it comes to your story. Depending on the circumstances and severity of the trauma, it may be hard for others to accept your notion to forgive, let alone finding forgiveness themselves. So it's good to have it in your head for a potential outcome so that you can equip yourself with how you'll respond. If you choose to forgive, it's because you know that it'll serve you greater in the long run than it would be to seek revenge or hold onto resentment. Some of your loved ones around you may have their feet placed very firmly in the ground of hate, resentment, or some other type of response that ultimately causes more harm than good. I know that if my dad were to be alive today and he knew I had completely forgiven my grandad, he would have seen it as a betrayal. But that's only because he hadn't found forgiveness himself, and he was living in a world full of hate. So be strong in your decision if you do decide to find forgiveness. Explain your reasoning to a loved one if they ask, and hopefully, they'll see a side to the situation they also might want to join you with. However, if that isn't the case, then that's fine. Everyone has their own belief system and their own story. Everyone doesn't need to agree with you, the way you don't need to agree with everyone else. So just stand firm in your decision and ask that they respect it.

Lastly, another perspective you could shift your focus towards when it comes to forgiveness is understanding that whatever decision you made at that time, was one you needed to make to get you to where you are today. It was done for a reason. You kept silent for a reason. You left your job for a reason. You broke someone's heart for a reason. Whatever it was, you did it for a reason. You did the best that you could for where you were. I could easily sit here and continue to regret speaking up about the abuse, or I could forgive myself because I knew I kept silent for a reason. I kept silent because I was manipulated. I kept silent because I was scared. I kept silent because at the time it felt like the right thing to do. In the same way that when it came to breaking my silence, it felt like the right thing to do. Be grateful that you have been silent because it's brought you to a place right now, reading this book, with a desire to move beyond it and start changing things. Forgiveness is a magical tool that you can use when and where you please. If you want my advice, allow it to be one of the biggest values.

EXERCISE

Use the spaces below to answer each question as best you can.

Is forgiveness something that comes easy to you? What is your experience with it?

Have you forgiven yourself yet? If so, why did you choose to? If not, why not?

Is forgiving your abuser something that you feel like you need to do?

Practical Exercise A

I want you to go and stand in front of a mirror and say to that person staring back at you that you forgive them. Don't just mutter the words, mean that. Feel the forgiveness. If you want to, say "I forgive you for..." and fill in the ending. I want you to keep doing this until you notice changes being made. Oftentimes when we can't forgive ourselves, we find it hard to look in the mirror because it shows our true self, the one from which we hideaway. So let's change that.

Practical Exercise B

(optional)

If you are open to forgiving the abuser, I simply want you to allow yourself to understand that person's worldview and belief system. Understand why they did that to you. I know it's not always possible, but if you can, try to find out actual information about their story. Talk to family members who may know the abuser's background. Or if they are still around, sit down with them and ask. Build a story of that person which you'll find, as it did to me, it'll allow you to be open to forgiveness towards that person and the situation as a whole.

Letting Go

"If you realize that all things change, there is nothing you will try to hold on to. If you are not afraid of dying, there is nothing you cannot achieve." - *Lao Tzu*

When we don't let go of something, we are constantly beating the drum of that problem or event that took place. We are constantly living in a place of resistance. Or rather, we are constantly living in the past rather than truly experiencing the present moment. Can you think back to a time, perhaps very recently, where you were so engrossed in what you were doing that it almost seemed like nothing outside of it existed? Right, because in that brief period of time you were present in that moment. If you can constantly live in that state of 'living in the moment', then you'll find that naturally, you will let go of that thing you were attached to. Throughout my years of silence, I was constantly living from a place of resistance. Constantly thinking back to the events and operating from a place of negativity, or rather a place of low frequency. Which completely goes against who we are as human beings. We are meant to be operating at a frequency of which is our highest level. So when we think negative thoughts which then create negative emotions within our body, that is our body telling us that we are operating out of alignment with the frequency we need to be at. I remember when I went through a breakup which absolutely crushed me to pieces. For months I was begging the universe to bring her back. I was constantly questioning why she had left. Everything I saw and every song I heard was some type of trigger to her leaving, which had me living in a state of constant emotional negativity. I wanted so badly to find the solution without realising that you cannot find a solution from the same frequency where the problem was created. Only when I made a continuous effort to focus on myself did it raise the frequency I was operating from, thus allowing me to think and see more clearly. Which was the exact point where I was able to let go.

There is great power in detachment. Buddha once said, "*attachment is the source of all suffering.*" Especially when the thing we are attached to is the version of us that went through abuse and is keeping it secret. For me to break my silence, I knew that I couldn't do it from the version of me who was still attached and operating from the same frequency that experiences constant negative emotions. Why? Because breaking my silence would feel like it goes against every bone in my body. It's like I'm betraying the identity that I've lived as since the abuse happened. I remember when I read a quote by Robin Sharma which changed the game for me, and that was, "*what you focus on grows, what you think about expands, and what you dwell upon determines your destiny.*" It made me realise that because I was easily triggered and frequently thought about the abuse, it would continually grow and manifest into more of the same train of thought. What you believe creates your reality. So if you constantly believe you are ugly, shy, fat, to blame for what happened, can't be in a relationship because you don't trust easily, or anything else that is self-sabotaging, then that will become your reality. Hence why most people who live with their story buried deep down, over time, deteriorate and get worse (my dad for example).

So then it begs the question, how do you let go? Well, you have to shift yourself into a higher frequency so that you can let go. You have to start thinking about different thoughts to start creating different emotions within you. You have to shift the focus from *"I blame myself"* to *"I am not to blame"* From *"I can't forgive that person"* to *"finding forgiveness is allowing me to be emotionally free"*. Try to shift your focus and see the events that happened to you as something that allowed you to turn into the person that you are today. I say quite often that being sexually abused and the death of my father are some of the best things that happened to me, much like Jacob Kauffman in his story. I don't for a second mean to undermine what happened to you or say that you need to see it as a great thing. Please, that's not what I'm getting at. However, I say it because being sexually abused has created the person that I am today, with a purpose that has led me to write this book and helping countless people break their silence. It's allowed me to have thick skin and face adversity with my head held high. If I weren't abused then I wouldn't be doing any of this. Today I have a strong mentality and can thrive when my back is against the wall when there is nowhere to run because of what I went through. With my father's death, if he were still alive today I wouldn't have broken my silence with the world. Whilst in one breath I would love for my father to be alive today, in another breath, I chose to use that event to serve me. But I could only bring myself to allow those events to serve me when I started to operate from a higher frequency and let go of the hold it had over me. So when it comes to letting go, think about where your focus is, because whatever you focus on you feel. And whatever you consistently feel you start to create momentum with. So the key is breaking that pattern and outgrowing that identity that isn't serving you. When you let go of that which is not serving you, you then let in of that which does.

So when you catch yourself thinking or feeling something negative, I first want you to be proud of the fact you have the awareness around that thought or feeling. Then realise that it's a good thing because it's showing you who you are not. You are not the version of you who lives every day with shame, guilt and fear clouding over you because of what happened. You are not someone who is meant to be living in a low frequency and vibrational state. So if you can catch yourself every time this happens and allow yourself to experience the emotions flooding through you, you can make the conscious decision to just let that go.

The last thing I would like to mention is about faith. I'm no religious man, but if you haven't gathered already, I'm a very spiritual man. I believe that the universe is a powerful force that shows us the way if we allow it to. Our ego is the opposite. Our ego wants to control every little detail in our lives. It wants to be in control of our emotions, it wants to control how we meet our future partner, and it wants to control how we deal with our traumas. Which means we are attached to the outcome of everything we do, thus living in resistance. Rather than doing something with no expectation of an outcome because we know that if it's meant to be, the universe will allow it to happen. Which is such a freeing way to live life. It allows us to operate from our greater being because it causes us to just BE rather than seek out something that allows us to have (i.e. be love as opposed to seeking love from someone else.) So knowing that the way you have been doing things since the abuse isn't serving you, you should instead put your trust into the universe that letting go will direct you to a place for which will serve you for the greater good. Trust that the universe will bring you what you need when you need it.

EXERCISE

Use the spaces below to answer each question as best you can.

Are there parts of you that you know you are holding onto which do not serve you? If so, what are they?

What are some beliefs you have which do not serve you? Write the new belief next to it (*Example: "I'm not loved" - "I am filled with love and attract it wherever I go".)*

Do you feel like your ego has had more control over you than you'd like? If so, in what ways?

Practical Exercise

I want you to start being conscious and aware of the feelings in your body when you are triggered. When you think back to the part of your story where the abuse happened, I want you to witness the motions your body is going through, but then I want you to say in your head "I'm letting you go". And consciously let it go and feel it melt away. Do this consistently and you'll find that it becomes less and less frequent.

Masculinity

"The crisis facing our boys today is not masculinity, rather it is toxic patriarchal hyper-masculinity. In many ways, our boys are constantly clashing within themselves between who they really are and who they are expected to be. The stress of guarding and protecting a false self creates a deep wound in the male psyche." - Melia Keeton Digby

I want to talk quickly about masculinity before we move forward. This section will be valuable for both men and women. Women, so they can better understand the men in their life. And for the men, so they can better understand themselves.

As I mentioned earlier in this book, my dad was constantly asserting his dominance. He continuously branded himself as an 'alpha' male. He took steroids whilst bodybuilding, he made questionable decisions when it came to money, he wouldn't let people talk down to him, and always had to be in control. Because he was my role-model, I followed in the same shoes. And because of this, I grew up subconsciously driven by this perception of being alpha. I was ready to throw punches if it were called for, I thought I was better than everyone else and I thought I deserved whatever I asked for. If something didn't go my way, or someone treated me like dirt, then I would go into defensive mode. But here is where I want you to really take note. I went into defensive mode because what was really happening was my perception of what it meant to be a man, this identity, had been challenged. I was made to feel *'less than'*. My ego was taking a battering and was causing serious internal damage. For so many years I thought I was strong, and while I may have seemed that way to people who only saw the shell of me I was, in fact, weak. I was asserting my masculinity to hide what I lacked. And this is the same reason many more women will be reading this book as opposed to men. Because a lot of men live in a world where they're invincible. They are wearing a mask which is glued tight, and even coming to the idea of picking up this book challenges their ego. It highlights to them an area of themselves which they've grown to ignore and detach themselves from. Women are much better at acknowledging those areas, embracing them and communicating them. Whereas for us men, it's the opposite. Primarily due to society, and also their own father figures. So they become very good at using their physical abilities to dominate, control and come out on top. And whilst this may work for a considerable amount of time, it'll come a time where that won't be needed anymore, especially for survivors. My dad buried his story of abuse really deep, often overcompensating in external measures (money, success and status) to make up for the areas of lack that were formed from his childhood wounds. But he grew tired of running and his past demons caught up with him. Alcohol then became the replacement, sending him down a dark road ultimately leading to his death.

I'm not for one second saying that us men shouldn't be masculine, because I believe we should. However, I believe that we need to be aware of the areas we are trying to overcompensate for. Male survivors of abuse, especially sexual, feel like their manhood was taken from them by the abuser. Trauma robs you of the feeling that you are in-charge of yourself. Which is why men then start to overcompensate by seeking status and validation in the external world, because they lack it in their internal world. This quest that men go on is linked to insecurity and fear because we tend to hold value in the thoughts and judgements of others. Which is the main reason survivors don't break their silence. It's also the main reason male suicides are alarmingly high. I don't look at my dad's death as suicide, however, I don't think it was far from it. His heart gave up before his will to live did, that's all. This is why I'm writing this book and screaming my message from the rooftops. To not only help every survivor break their silence but help change the masculine stereotype and get more men to be open and vulnerable.

EXERCISE

Use the spaces below to answer each question as best you can.

Do you feel like your false sense of masculinity has had a part in keeping you silent?

Did you have a father figure growing up? If so, have you subconsciously followed in their footsteps when it comes to being a man?

In what ways do you feel like your abuse has damaged your masculine identity? And in what ways do you think you've tried to fill that lack through the external world?

Practical Exercise

On a piece of paper, I want you to write down what you fear will happen once you break your silence. On a new piece of paper, I want you to write the opposite, this will be your new and positive reality of what will happen once you share your story. Now I want you to get your old piece of paper, then one with the old belief, and I want you to burn it from existence. That's no longer your reality.

Self-Love

"Be gentle with yourself, learn to love yourself, to forgive yourself, for only as we have the right attitude toward ourselves can we have the right attitude toward others."
- Wilfred Peterson

If there was just ONE thing you could take away from this book that I believe would not only serve you greatly in breaking your silence but also for the rest of your life, is the practice of self-love. For many people who have been sexually abused, their internal love-tank was destroyed. Growing up they were constantly seeking love from others because the love that they gave themselves was running dry. Especially if they believe they were to blame, or they don't like who looks back at them in the mirror because they feel disgusted with themselves. For someone who is living in that state, the act of self-love is extremely hard to practise. Which makes an unfortunate breakup with the one we love almost unbearable because it feels like they have taken away every ounce of love you once felt. I know that feeling all too well as I've mentioned already. I remember when I first heard about self-love. I automatically assumed that I did love myself, but after seeing how I responded to multiple events in my life, it was quite evident that I didn't. So I started to do all the activities that I thought would make me happy, as I believed this would allow me to get in touch with my love-tank so that I could start filling it up. But I soon came to realise that it's not about doing extra things on the 'to-do' list. It's not about piling things in, it's more so about letting go of what doesn't serve you. So once you start to action some of the things I mentioned in the 'Letting Go' chapter of this book, then you'll notice that you start to feel more love because it's already being generated inside of you. Since we were born, we have been conditioned to not love ourselves. We have been told not to make too much noise, to stop expressing ourselves, to not chase this career path because there's no guarantee of success, and to stop being selfish. I have spent many years in the fitness industry and the biggest red flag I saw with my clients was their lack of self-love. They wanted to lose weight because they'd compare themselves to the latest Instagram model. They would want to put on more muscle so they could feel more masculine. Adverts for pills and shakes out to the masses for rapid weight loss, with this constant notion of quick-fixes for people's insecurities. But if we could just operate from a place of unconditional love towards ourselves, then we wouldn't need to be chasing after this external desire because the desire would already be fulfilled from within. All of this is conditioning that we've been subconsciously living throughout life, thus creating the identities we are today. Ones that feel broken and less than. Which as you know by now is not who you truly are. So when it comes to practising self-love, the way to do this is by taking on-board everything you are learning in this book. Forgive yourself for what happened and forgive the abuser too if you wish.

Looking back, my self-love really grew when I stopped portraying the parts of me which protected my insecurities. When I allowed myself to take off my masks and show my true self to the world, that was when I started to love myself because I was just being me. With nothing to prove and nothing to hide. I loved myself for being me. Which in return allowed other people to love me in the same way. But their love only compliments the love I already have for myself, it doesn't fill up where there is a lack of.

My last take on self-love is gratefulness. When you can become grateful for what you have and who you are, you'll see it spill over into every area of your life. Linking back to Robin Sharma's quote about what you put your focus on will grow, if you focus more on what you are grateful for in life, you'll then create the thoughts and emotions to go along with it. So when it comes to thinking about what happened in the past or what's going to happen in the future, they will be in alignment with the feeling of gratitude that you feel in the present moment.

There were times where I'd splash out a fortune on Ralph Lauren and I'd walk out with the biggest smile. I'd feel on top of the world. But compared to the level of internal happiness that I have now? There is no comparison. Because every day I wake up and I'm filled with immediate gratitude. Well, most of the time. Albeit I'm a human being and not a robot. So if there comes a morning where I am slow and groggy, and the positive energy is a little dim, then my morning gratitude meditation sorts it out. Because here's the thing, we already have everything we need. The universe gives us what we already have. It gives us more love as we are already filled with love, and it gives us more energy as we are already filled with energy. Which then translates into new opportunities for growth because we are open to it. So if you can shift your focus away from all the things you have done wrong in life, away from the abuse, away from the parts of you that you do not like, and put the focus onto positive energy, then you'll see your life radically transform.

EXERCISE

Use the spaces below to answer each question as best you can.

Out of 100%, how much is your love-tank filled up to? Be honest. Why?

In what ways have you attempted to seek love from outside yourself?

In what ways do you show love towards yourself currently? What could you start doing?

Practical Exercise

Think back to a time in your life where you felt extremely loved. This could be with a family member, a partner at the time, or by yourself. I want you to take yourself there. Who are you with? Where are you? What are you wearing? What sounds can you hear? What can you smell? What are you feeling? Really take time to think about what you are feeling. Allow these emotions of love to flow through you. Now allow the colours in the picture to get brighter. Allow the sounds to get louder. Allow the picture to get bigger. Now I want you to look through the eyes of that version of you who felt loved in that moment. I want you to tap into this feeling and draw upon it whenever you need it. This is a feeling of love that should be coming from within at all times, not of which someone else is giving you.

I also want you to write out 3 new things you are grateful for every single morning, and every single evening. Make this consistent and part of your daily routine.

Shifting Your Identity

"Never mind searching for who you are. Search for the person you aspire to be." - Robert Brault

Numerous times in this book I have talked about our 'identity'. Just to clarify, our identity is our current version of ourselves, it's our self-image that we have today. So if today you are someone who operates out of lack, someone who is tied down by their past demons, and someone who has zero self-confidence, then this is your current identity. Which I'm sure you're fully aware is an identity you need to shift out of. Why? Because it's not serving you. It's not allowing you to operate at your highest frequency and be emotionally free. In the homework section of this chapter, I ask you to create an identity of your future self. It could be someone who has shared their story, who has found forgiveness, who moved out of the abusive household, who is truly happy, who serves the community, who's love tank is overflowing, who has a beautiful and loving family, and whatever else you wish to be part of that future version of you. You need to know where you want to go and who you want to be so that not only can you get there, but so you can also see how the current version of you is completely out of alignment with your future self. In the homework, I teach you what to do next after you've done this which is super powerful. But before we get to that I want you to understand the power of choice that you have within you. Just because you've lived in silence for some time doesn't mean that you need to continue to do so. Just because you blame yourself doesn't mean you need to continue to blame yourself. Just because you've realised you haven't been communicating with your inner child doesn't mean you can't change that. If you look back and think hard enough, I can guarantee a list full of examples where you tuned into your higher self (the place you are born to be operating from) and made tough choices. You made a decision that was brave and courageous. If you've made them before then you can certainly do it again. You have the power to break your silence. You have the power to completely let go of everything that doesn't serve you. You have the power to operate from your highest frequency and be the best version of yourself. Nothing or no one, not even the abuser, deserves to have a hold of you. So right now I want you to set the intention that you are going to shed your current identity and step into the shoes of the one that you're going to create in the homework section. This is called an identity shift, and it's something you are about to experience. If I have the absolute honour of meeting you at some point in the future, then I want to meet this new identity that you're about to create.

I believe that you'll do it, and so should you.

EXERCISE

Use the spaces below to answer each question as best you can.

List out 10 times in your life where you made a courageous decision

Do you believe you have the power to be anyone you want to be? Why?

What's stopping you from shifting identity and becoming your best self?

Practical Exercise

On one A4 piece of paper, I want you to draw yourself, feel free to let it be a stick figure or something more creative. I then want you to list everything you see and believe about yourself right now. Place each item in a bubble surrounding this person. I want you to list everything, which will more than likely include a load of self-sabotaging thoughts and actions. Then at the top in BOLD letters I want you to title it 'OLD IDENTITY'.

Then on a separate piece of A4 paper, I would like you to draw yourself again, but then list out everything of your future identity. List out all the positives and traits that DO serve you. Don't hold back on this. There are no limitations. So let your inner child run free. Once finished, I want you to label the top in BOLD letters 'NEW IDENTITY'.

I now want you to take your old identity sheet and burn it. Remove it from existence. Detach yourself from that version. It doesn't serve you. It's not you.

Then I want you to take your new identity sheet and set the intention that you are that person NOW. Write "THIS IS ME" at the top. Why? Because if you set this version of yourself as a 'goal' to get to, then you are telling the universe that you aren't there yet, which implies that you are operating from a place of lack. So BE that new identity. Sell yourself on the story that WILL serve you as opposed to the story you've been listening to. Keep this new identity worksheet somewhere you will see it all the time. Look at it when you wake up and before you go to sleep, along with doing your gratitude list.

Ways To Break Your Silence

"Your silence will not protect you" - *Audre Lorde*

When I say "break your silence", it's good to set the intention of verbally telling someone about what happened. However, I'm fully aware it is a huge first step to take for some people. Which is why I want to give you some examples of how you can maybe build yourself up to telling someone if that's the path that makes you feel most comfortable.

The first thing I want you to understand is that verbal communication is just a form of expression. In the same way that painting a picture, choreographing a dance piece or writing a piano song is. I simply chose to voice it through verbal communication straight off the bat because that was the path I wanted to take. You could take the same path, or pick one entirely different. Here, below I will share some ways you could express your story, to begin with:

- You could write a song to sing. Or you could write a piece of music using your favourite instrument that expresses how you feel.

- Do you like to draw or paint? Then why don't you draw a picture or experiment with paint on a blank canvas? This could be a great form of expression. Many painters create artwork for themselves as an expression of something they are currently going through. Which is why people buy them because they can relate to the artwork.
- If you like to dance, then choreographing a dance piece could be a great option for you. You could perform it just for you, or for others.
- What about clay moulding or knitting? This may seem a bit out there, but it's actually not. Not only are these very therapeutic, but for the end result, you could have created a piece of work that resembles a certain feeling you've had locked away for so many years.
- What works for a lot of people is writing. Just like some of the survivors above, you could write out your story. Whether that be on paper, on a google doc, in a journal, or on the 'Your Story' page earlier in this book. Speaking of journaling, you could take the option of simply writing how you feel every day. Sometimes once you write out your feelings on paper, you find that you can manage them better, allowing you to explore your story and take the next steps on breaking your silence.
- This may seem a tad unconventional, but joining a local boxing club or self-defence class may be a great option for you. Sometimes we have so many emotions stored inside of us, and a lot of them we can't even name. Hitting a punching bag every week may help you release emotion you never knew you had, allowing you to be more clear-headed and

comfortable in the next steps to take.

Do you see where I'm going with this? It's about grabbing the clogged up balls of feelings and emotions that you have buried down deep and allowing them to be expressed in whichever form resonates with you the most. So if you know that grabbing a paintbrush and allowing your emotions run wild would be useful to you, then do that. It's all about YOU right now. It's about moving you one step along. It's about doing whatever it takes to break your silence. You may find you need to start by drawing a picture that resembles your story, which then leads into a poem and then leads to you feeling safer to share it with your family. Who knows what the journey will look like for you, the key is about getting started.

Another option is voicing it out loud, but only to yourself. Which I strongly recommend trying to do, even whilst pursuing one of the options above. Because here's the thing about silence, it reinforces the isolation of abuse. You're allowing that trauma to thrive inside of you like a virus. But when you can just mutter the words *"I was raped by my uncle when I was 10 years old"* out loud into existence, it holds immense power. Let me give you an example. If I ever got into trouble growing up as a kid, my dad would send me to my room. He would take everything away from me and leave me with only pen and paper (which is probably why I'm such a good drawer come to think of it.) If I wanted to leave my bedroom for any reason at all, even if it was to go to the toilet, I had to ask. It's safe to say I spent a lot of alone time in my bedroom growing up. Fast forward 15 - 20 years or so, and I was a young adult who would much prefer to be on his own than socialise with his friends. I'd much rather stay on the sideline than be mixing around with other people, and I thought that was just the way I was. Sure I would prefer to be the person who was always socialising and building relationships with other people rather than being a hermit at home. But I sold myself on the story in which that version was someone who I couldn't become. But upon watching a random video on YouTube one day (as you do), I was watching someone tell a story which was pretty much similar to mine. It made me realise that my past neglect and abandonment as a child (oftentimes when I was being punished, the only way I could speak to my dad was via letter. Bearing in mind we lived in a small flat.) had carried through to the adult version of me. Once I realised this I didn't want to really acknowledge it because I didn't want people to think that my dad was a bad person, nor did I want to start thinking that. So I chose to have some type of awareness around it, but that was it. It was only once I voiced it out loud (I told my partner at the time, only because I had already spoken out about my abuse.) was I able to label it. Because once you give it a label, not only do you have a level of control over it, you can also start to separate it from you. It's almost like you are giving that certain behaviour, thought or feeling an identity from which you can start choosing to detach yourself from. It's only when you can bring yourself to say the words out loud (whether that's the first method you try or not) can you truly start the healing process.

EXERCISE

Use the spaces below to answer each question as best you can.

Are you ready to break your silence? Why?

In what way do you think you'll break your silence?

How do you feel right now?

Practical Exercise

It's time for you to break your silence. Do what feels right. Does this mean that you go and tell the world right now? Speak to a therapist? Paint a picture? That's completely down to you. But now is the time. So your practical work right now is to put this book down and take action on the method that feels right for you.

We Rescue Kids

125,000 followers and hundreds of messages later, an idea sparked. I reached out to a close friend who had already started to get the ball rolling on a new charity, and after some sleepless nights, Jeweliet Tangen, Samual Young and I joined forces to create We Rescue Kids (#WeRescueKids). At WRK, our primary goal is to rescue kids from sexual abuse. We know what it's like to not receive the right support as a victim of sexual abuse. Which is why our aftercare is where a lot of our energy and resources go, both through our safe homes and online therapy.

If you are a victim of sexual abuse are you're looking for support, then please reach out to us. We have a full team ready to welcome you with open arms. It's a judge-free zone. Just get ready for the love, because we have a lot of that to give :)

And if you are looking to help us in any way, whether that be to join the team or something else, then please reach out too. There is always space for those who want to be part of WRK.

Our contact details are below:

www.werescuekids.org / @werescuekids / info@werescuekids.org / +15315415437

Final Words

"There are so many ways to be brave in this world. Sometimes bravery involves laying down your life for something bigger than yourself, or for someone else. Sometimes it involves giving up everything you have ever known, or everyone you have ever loved, for the sake of something greater. But sometimes it doesn't. Sometimes it is nothing more than gritting your teeth through pain, and the work of every day, the slow walk toward a better life. That is the sort of bravery I must have now." - Veronica Roth

We've gone on quite the journey so far. I've probably made you laugh and cry in this book, as well as hopefully inspired to make a positive change and break your silence. The whole point of this book is writing something I wish I had available to read when I was suffering in silence. I wish I knew that I wasn't the only one. I wish I had known that I wasn't a freak, that I wasn't to blame and that I didn't deserve it. I won't lie to you, it was quite a surreal experience putting this book together. Partly because of the research and stories I dived into to put this together, but also because I never saw myself writing a book to help survivors break their silence. So this is proof to you that anything can be done once you set your mind to it. Absolutely anything.

I wanted a huge part of this book to be about showcasing the stories of other brave survivors. These survivors showed great strength and trusted me to give them a platform to share their story. So I'm hoping that from reading these stories and everything else here, that we have all inspired you and given you the permission needed to share your story. In whichever way you wish to share it. If you do go down the road of sharing it online, please make sure you tag me into it so I can show you my love and support. If you also want to share your story with me privately, feel free to message me on Instagram. I can't guarantee that I see it straight away, but I'll do my best to respond to it as soon as I can. I'll always be here to support you, and the same for every other survivor out there. We are brothers and sisters in arms.

Lastly, I'd love for you to pay this forward. Whether it be the message (#breakthesilence), giving a copy of this book to a friend or posting a picture of you with this book on social media (make sure to tag me in it). The sooner we can get as many people breaking their silence and to start healing their wounds, the sooner we can break the chain. That chain being those victims suffering in silence who pass on parts of their identity to their children. It's onto us to show up and serve in whichever way we can. It's up to us as a collective to break the global silence and heal together, as one.

Thanks for reading and being on this journey with me.

Much love, Perry Power.

Printed in Great Britain
by Amazon

21510969R00081